A History of

the Sunningdale

New Course

from the Golden Age to the Present Day

A History of
the Sunningdale
New Course

from the Golden Age to the Present Day

Adrian Pepper

ß

Belgravia Press

First published in the UK 2023 by Belgravia Press.

Belgravia Press, a division of Pepper Media Ltd

33 Gloucester Street, London SW1V 2DB

Hardback ISBN 978-0-9926757-3-8

Typesetting, layout and jacket design by bounford.com

Printed in Great Britain by Swallowtail Print.

Contents

Acknowledgements

This book arises from a conversation on the eighth fairway of Sunningdale's New Course in March 2023. I was describing to my playing partner how Tom Simpson's loop went in the other direction. As he stood over his golf ball and I continued to talk, he politely suggested that I should write it all down.

What you find here is by no means a comprehensive account of the hundred years of the life of the New Course. I did not interview many dozens of golfers and club members alive today who would no doubt have had their own stories to tell of what has taken place down the years, both on the golf course and in Committee. My aim is to tell the story of how the course came into being and of the characters who played a significant part in its evolution. Events which are recounted are drawn from the published works of established golf writers, news reports and the archives of the club; any errors in their interpretation are my own.

I am much obliged to Sunningdale's Managing Director Tristan Hall for allowing me access to club archives, to Stephen Toon for his 1950 Robert Browning New Course guide, to Donald Steel for his recollections, to Kevin Diss and Simon Haines for providing images from their libraries;

and to all those who have left written works behind, not least Bernard Darwin, Tom Simpson, Henry Longhurst, Guy Bennett, Jimmy Sheridan, John Whitfield and John Churchill. I would like to thank Ron Sandler for suggesting I write this and Devika Malik for being such a fantastic partner, and not just on the course.

Those who play the New Course at Sunningdale regularly will identify more easily with the hole layouts, greens and hazards described in this book; but I hope the read will also be accessible to those who are not as familiar with the course who take pleasure from learning about the history of heathland golf.

Sunningdale is a golf club which teems with human life all year round, and each day the New Course hosts its share of drama, stress, laughter, despair and delight. Every golfer, caddie and spectator who has walked Harry Colt's fairways will have their own memories of special days out. We know how privileged we are to have played on such an exquisite piece of golfing country and we are indebted to those who gave their time and effort over the past century to make it so.

Adrian Pepper
November 2023

CHAPTER 1

H.S. Colt

O n 19 July 1901, Harry Shapland Colt travelled from Hastings to London to attend a meeting at the Café Monico on Shaftesbury Avenue with the Committee of Sunningdale Golf Club. A year before, he had applied unsuccessfully for the job of Secretary of the Royal and Ancient Golf Club of St Andrews. Now he was one of five candidates being interviewed, from 435 applicants, for the newly created post of Sunningdale Golf Club Secretary.

Colt, who had served as the Honorary Secretary of Rye Golf Club for the previous five years, performed well and was acknowledged by the Committee as the outstanding candidate. He was offered the job. H.S. Colt resigned from his Hastings law firm, taking an 80 per cent pay cut for a salary of £150 per annum, and moved to Sunningdale to embark upon a new career in golf at the age of 32.

Garden G. Smith noted in the *Tatler*[1] that Mr Colt was "a member of the Royal and Ancient, the Oxford and Cambridge Golfing Society, and he is a member of the Rules

---

1   7 August 1901.

of Golf Committee. As Mr Colt has considerable experience of secretarial work in connection with the Rye Club, and is personally most popular, the appointment seems to be a fortunate one."

Born in Highgate, London in 1869, young Harry had moved with his mother and his five older siblings to Malvern after the death of his father when he was just two. He was taught how to play golf by Douglas Rolland, a Scottish professional who was the uncle of James Braid, at The Worcestershire Golf Club. Colt became an accomplished player,

Colt in his golfing prime.
Cigarette card, 1890s.

captaining the Cambridge University team in 1889 and winning the R&A's Jubilee Vase in 1891 and 1893. In 1894, Colt and his mentor Rolland made significant alterations to the course that had been laid out the previous year[2] on the links land of Rye. He spent the next six years gradually tweaking the course, developing his design philosophies.

---

2   The original course at Rye was laid out by Ramsay Hunter and Peter Paxton in 1893.

Colt was enthusiast for the idea that links-style golf could be recreated inland and was impressed by the course that had been built on the sandy heathlands at Sunningdale in 1900 by Willie Park Junior. Unlike many courses built inland at that time, Park's Sunningdale course made use of the natural features of the landscape and followed the principles of strategic golf design, setting it apart from the more penal layouts that were the hallmark of established golf course designers of the time[3].

Once installed as Secretary, Colt soon became instrumental in making changes to the course, for example by changing some of the sites of greens and bunkers and by lengthening some of the holes in response to the arrival of the rubber cored "Haskell" ball which flew much further than the "gutty". He also reworked the eight holes that E.E. (Ernest) Villiers had laid out next to the Dormy House to create the 18 short holes of Sunningdale Ladies Golf Club. Colt developed a passion for heathland golf and was soon to become involved in designing and refining other courses, work he performed alongside his secretarial duties at Sunningdale.

Colt started his architectural practice with Charles Hugh Alison in 1906. The following year, he travelled to Leeds to provide a second opinion on the newly completed Alwoodley Golf Club, which had been designed by Dr Alister Mackenzie.

---

3   The layouts of Old Tom Morris and the brothers Willie and Tom Dunn provide examples of the late Victorian penal style of course design.

This was the first time that Colt and Mackenzie had met, and they began a collaboration in the golf course design business which was formalised after the Great War and lasted until Mackenzie's departure from the partnership in 1923.

In the seven years before war broke out in 1914, Colt designed Kingsthorpe, Stoke Poges, Denham, Leamington and County, Newquay, Northamptonshire County, Swinley Forest, Betchworth Park, Blackmoor, St George's Hill, Brokenhurst Manor, Burhill, Camberley Heath, Copt Heath, Beaconsfield, Dun Laoghaire in Dublin, Puerta de Hierro in Madrid, St Cloud in Paris and the Eden Course at St Andrews.

In 1911, he visited North America, where he designed the Toronto Golf Club course and made his first visit to Pine Valley in Pennsylvania; and in 1913, he returned to the US to work with Donald Ross on Old Elm in Illinois and to design Detroit Country Club's course in Michigan. At the beginning of June that year, he spent a week with George Crump working on green locations and hole routing at Pine Valley[4]. In Canada, he designed Pine Ridge, Manitoba and Hamilton, Ontario, including the Ladies' nine hole course there.

Colt, Alison and Mackenzie were all university-educated amateur golfers who represented a new breed of golf course designer. Their designs catered for the needs and abilities

---

4   Specifically, he got Crump across the river at Pine Valley with the creation of the daunting one shot fifth hole. After Crump's death in 1918, Colt and his partner Hugh Alison continued to contribute improvements to the design of the Pine Valley course.

of handicap golfers as well as the best players. They were advocates of strategic golf design, a school which rejected the idea of forcing golfers to make long carries over penal hazards and instead espoused the advantages of offering alternative routes to the green. They took their inspiration from the Old Course at St Andrews in its widened form[5] – a course which positioned hazards over the shorter route to the green but gave options to the weaker player to avoid having to carry the ball over penal hazards and so play a course within their own level of ability. Courses which provided more than one route the green could be played by players of all abilities, and it is no coincidence that more people took up the game at a time when the courses being built were becoming less penal.

Colt put an end to the Victorian era of penal golf course construction. Before Colt, holes were straight and all shaped like the letter 'i', only differing from each other by their length. Colt's business partner Hugh Alison observed:

"There was only one form of bunker. This consisted of a rampart built of sods with a trench in front of it filled with a sticky substance, usually dark red in colour. The face of the rampart was perpendicular. It was precisely 3ft 6 inches in height throughout, and ran at an exact right angle to the line of play... There were no side hazards except long grass and

---

5   The Old Course at St Andrews was widened by Allan Robertson in 1848 to provide alternate routes of play.

13

trees. The fairway was invariably rectangular, and
the putting greens were square and flat. Some clubs
could not afford to make all their putting greens
quite flat, but in such cases the host would apologise
to his guest when an undulating green was reached."

Colt totally changed the aspect of golf courses, designing
them in tune with natural features of the land. He forced
golfer to think, obliging them to ask themselves at what point
they could cut short a curve or how they could make use of
a contour. He positioned tees on elevated ground, set back
behind modest stretches of rough, pointed at wide, curving
fairways leading to pear-shaped, often-elevated greens,
protected by carefully sited bunkers. He positioned bunkers
in thought-provoking positions and at angles which no longer
penalised the poor topped shot of the weaker player. Colt was
meticulous in his approach to setting up the course's strategic
challenges. He pioneered the use of the drawing board and is
credited with bringing an academic side to golf architecture.

He served as Sunningdale Secretary until 1911, at
which point he had become so busy with his architectural
commitments that he relinquished the administrative side of
the role, becoming Joint Secretary responsible for oversight of
all matters involving golf and the courses. In 1913, he reduced
his involvement further, resigning as Joint Secretary and
attending Green Committee meetings only.

Soon after the Great War began, Colt came back as Acting
Secretary, a post he occupied until September 1917, from

14

The Sunningdale Committee 1910. Club Secretary HS Colt is standing in the middle row on the far right.

which point he was to devote all his organisational skills to the war effort, having been appointed Assistant Food Commissioner for the Southern Division of England.

The Club's founder T.A. Roberts took over as Hon Secretary and E.E. Villiers agreed to assist in supervising the course, which was being maintained by a reduced green staff of three and the voluntary efforts of local ladies. Colt was to be paid an honorarium for his advice as and when needed. H.S. Colt's contribution to the Club was recognised in June 1918, when he was made an Honorary Life Member.

CHAPTER 2

Origins of the New: The Nine Hole

The Sunningdale estate is a good example of lowland heath, one of the most ancient British landscapes. The land in antiquity was part of the Windsor Forest, which became a royal hunting ground soon after the accession of William the Conqueror in 1066. In the Middle Ages, most of the property on which the golf courses sits today belonged to the Benedictine Nunnery of Broomhall. In 1524, title to the land was acquired for St John's College Cambridge by John Fisher, Bishop of Rochester (acting as executor for Lady Margaret Beaufort, the mother of Henry VII) and the land was farmed or grazed over the following four centuries. The estate appears on nineteenth century maps[6] as being located on the far eastern fringe of the parish of Windlesham, the boundary with the parish of Old Windsor falling on what is today the A30 London Road.

---

6   Walter (H), Map of Windsor Forest, 1 August 1823.

The leases acquired by the Golf Club from St John's College Cambridge in 1900 consisted of three farms (Broomhall Farm, Titlarks Farm and Stavehall Waste) plus unfarmed land containing pine, gorse and heather. The freehold interest in that land remains in the possession of St John's College to this day. To the south and east of the St John's College land lay Chobham Common, owned at that time by the Earl of Onslow[7].

There were already a few golf holes laid on the land occupied by the 16th, 17th and 18th holes of what became the Ladies course,[8] before Sunningdale Golf Club came into existence. Three years before the leases were acquired for the formation of the Club, in 1897, two brothers, T.A. (Tom) and G.A. Roberts, built a house on a bridle path which ran up the hill from Sunningdale railway station to Valley End. They called the house Ridgemount[9], and the road became known as Ridgemount Road.

Willie Park's 18 hole Sunningdale Golf Club layout was to be found on the land above Ridgemount Road and opened for play in 1901. On the land below Ridgemount Road, Colt extended the Sunningdale Ladies course, which had first opened for play in 1902. Ladies' golf enjoyed a boom in

---

7   The Earldom was created in 1801 for George Onslow, 4th Baron Onslow, whose antecedent Arthur Onslow had been created a Baronet in 1674.

8   Today known as Sunningdale Heath Golf Club.

9   Today, Ridgemount is the Dormy House Care Home.

Ridgemount, built by the Roberts brothers, had been extended and had become the Dormy House by the time this photo was taken in 1915.

popularity at least as great as the gentlemen's game during the Edwardian era.

At a time of widespread peace and prosperity, affluent English families were looking for new ways to enjoy their leisure time and the fashion for playing golf spread rapidly. In the spring of 1911, the Sunningdale Golf Club Committee was approached by some residents of the neighbourhood to ask if the Club would let another portion of the land leased from St John's, which was not used, to establish a nine hole golf course for the use of residents.

The Committee took the view that, rather than run a nine hole course itself, it should be run by a separate organisation, with members of Sunningdale Golf Club able to join the club on favourable terms (at £2 2s per annum with no entrance fee, as opposed to £3 3s per annum). A referendum notice sent by the Sunningdale Golf Club Secretary H.S. Colt to members in June 1911 indicated that the land had been surveyed to establish the feasibility of a nine hole course and invited them to vote on a proposal to lease the land for an annual rent of £2 an acre. There was overwhelming support for the new scheme, and construction of the new nine hole course at Sunningdale got underway.

H.S. Colt, who was at that time busy on numerous other golf course design projects, laid out these holes over ground starting and finishing on the current practice ground and covering the area around Titlarks Hill:

- The first hole on this course covered the same land as the first hole on the New today
- The second went south in the direction of Chobham over the land occupying today's seventeeth hole a little way down today's sixteenth
- The third was a shorter but almost identical version of the third on today's New course
- The fourth was straight hole onto today's fifteenth fairway to a green some 100 yards short and 60 yards left of the present green, the site being now completely in the trees
- The fifth was a short hole from forward of today's sixteenth tee to a green on the elbow of today's sixteenth fairway
- The sixth was a long par four east (behind the homes on the south side of Titlarks Hill Road)
- The seventh was a 200 yard par 3 north, in the angle of Titlarks Hill Road and Chobham Road

- The eighth involved crossing Titlarks Hill Road and ran 300 yards alongside the north side of the road over the shoulder of the hill at the back of the current practice ground
- The ninth headed back across today's practice ground to a green short of the Artisans' clubhouse.

It was named Sunningdale Heath Golf Club (but covered none of the ground of the course known as Sunningdale Heath Golf Club today) and was colloquially known as the Nine 'Ole. The chauffeurs of members of Sunningdale Golf Club could play at the Nine 'Ole and be back at the car in time to pick up those who had been playing 18 holes at Sunningdale Golf Club, and so over time the course also became known as Chauffeurs' Course.

Claude Harris, golf course contractor, 1913. Credit: Golf Chronicle

The course was built by the construction company G.A. Franks Harris Bros, Ltd of Guildford, Surrey. Colt had persuaded one of the brothers who owned the company to set up a specialist golf construction division, which was then manned by foremen recruited from existing golf club staffs. The head of the golf construction division, C.D. (Claude) Harris, himself played to a handicap of one.

An article which appeared in an obscure golf journal[10] in 1913 explained, "C.D. Harris steps in when H.S. Colt steps out. One could describe the latter as a designer of golf courses, the former as the man who comes after and puts Mr Colt's ideas into effect." Claude Harris told the interviewer:

> "Perhaps it was my meeting with Mr Colt that turned the attention of the firm towards the construction of golf courses, for he had just planned out a new nine hole course at Sunningdale, which is known as the Sunningdale Heath Golf Club, and I was asked whether we could undertake construction for it...Well as I said we made a nine hole golf course at Sunningdale, and Mr Colt has been good enough to recommend me for plenty of work since. That Sunningdale course had to be completed in six weeks, and we got through it in time. We put 350 men onto it, under some good ganger men, and I practically acted as a foreman. That was my first experience of dealing with heather and, if it makes the work harder, it has its compensating advantages, for a heather course always looks better than anything else..."

---

10 Golfchronicle.wordpress.com, Claude D Harris: Maker of courses, 30/5/19, Lee Patterson.

The Nine Hole course was open to members of the public on payment of a green fee; it made enough money to pay the wages of one greenkeeper to take care of it. It did not contain many bunkers to maintain, but there was a lot of mowing involved.

During the Great War, golf continued to be played, but Sunningdale Heath Golf Club fell into financial difficulties and a decision was taken soon after the end of the war to return its land to Sunningdale Golf Club. At the centre of the land deal was the Founder of Sunningdale Golf Club, the Trustee of Sunningdale Heath Golf Club and the Agent for St John's College[11], T.A. Roberts, who conveniently had a foot in all three camps.

In August 1919, the Trustees of the Heath Club (F.A. Govett and T.A. Roberts) wrote to the Heath Club's debenture holders, explaining that despite the waiving of rent and the payment of liberal contributions on the part of neighbouring residents, they judged the Debentures to have very little, if any, realisable value.

"On the other hand," the letter continued, "the Committee of Sunningdale Golf Club recognise there is a considerable amount of substantial value in the course as it stands for the purposes which they contemplate," and the Trustees recommended acceptance of the offer to purchase the

---

11 TA Roberts had in 1914 been appointed by St John's College to replace a Mr Kirle as the College's agent, a position he held until 1944 when he was succeeded by his brother George.

Debentures of Sunningdale Heath Golf Club for 25 per cent of their face value.

The purpose for which they contemplated was the elimination of the seventh and eight holes of the Nine Hole, releasing the land for the development of several new homes on Titlarks Hill, and so raise funds to purchase new land on Chobham Common on which a new 18 hole course could be built.

On September 1st 1919, E.E. Villiers, the Hon Secretary of Sunningdale Heath Golf Club wrote to members explaining that the debenture holders had accepted Sunningdale Golf Club's offer and "I have in consequence to inform you that this Club will cease to exist from September 30th, when the course will be taken over by Sunningdale Golf Club".

But that was not the end for the Nine Hole. In 1923, it was decided that new holes would be constructed for the Nine Hole on land not used for the New Course, and members of the former Heath Club could retain their playing rights. In 1929, Sunningdale Golf Club offered owners of houses adjoining the Nine Hole an annual badge for the price of two guineas giving every member of the household (including staff) playing rights on it.

One of those residents was H.O. Sillem, who built a house (known then as Parkers Hill, now Park Hill) off the Chobham Road behind which the sixth hole ran. His son Stephen, a member of the club for most of the twentieth century, grew up there before the house was sold to fellow member

J.R.A. (John) Stroyan[12]. In a memoir that S.G. (Stephen) Sillem wrote for the club in the mid-1980s, he described the sixth as "a long and splendid hole (my private practice ground) which ran from a tee at the corner of the garden of the house on the right of the 16th (New) fairway. A fine wide fairway with cross bunkers about 275 yards from the tee, running along the bottom of the gardens that had then been built on Titlarks Hill to a slightly raised green which was roughly mid-way between Stearn's Farm and Parkers Hill. This entire hole has disappeared under an impenetrable jungle of trees, thorns and bushes."

The reconstructed Nine Hole course would continue in use until December 1937, when holes 1 and 9 were taken back by the Club to create a practice ground. Soon after the outbreak of war in 1939, the Nine Hole was closed for good.

---

12 Captain JRA Stroyan was a barrister, South African Breweries magnate and patron of the men's and ladies' amateur game.

CHAPTER 3
Colt's New Design

After the Great War, golf enjoyed a renaissance. Peace, combined with a dramatic increase in car ownership, heralded the start of a new golfing boom.[13] At Sunningdale, F.P. Le Marchand was appointed Secretary in March 1919 from a field of 350 applicants, taking the reins at a club whose membership figures were recovering rapidly.[14]

To accommodate an increasingly active membership, the Club could make use of several holes of the original Nine Hole, as well as additional land on Chobham Common (where holes four to fifteen would be situated) to build a new 18 hole course. The newly acquired Chobham Common land consisted of 168 acres of freehold title purchased from the Earl of Onslow, in a deal masterminded by Lord Dunedin, an eminent lawyer and former Cabinet Minister who was

---

13 The twenties witnessed new 36 hole layouts constructed to the east of Sunningdale at Wentworth in 1924 and on Crown land to the west of Sunningdale at The Berkshire in 1928.

14 By mid-1919 there were 577 members and rising, compared with 762 in 1913, the year before war had broken out.

Captain of the Club between 1921 and 1923[15]. The Club today marks his contribution to the founding of the New Course by playing a handicap medal competition in July each year for the Dunedin Cup.

After the Green Committee had asked James Braid for his advice on the feasibility of using the newly acquired land for a golf course, a Special General Meeting was held in July 1921 to approve a resolution to proceed.

H.S. Colt was appointed architect. As a golf course designer, 52 year old Colt was at the top of his game. He had gone back into the golf course design business at the end of Great War and was now in partnership with Dr Alister Mackenzie as well as Hugh Alison. He now could draw on them both for advice and ideas, as he prepared to

Andrew Graham Murray, the first Viscount Dunedin, who oversaw the land purchase. Painting by Sir James Guthrie (1859–1930).

---

15 Later, the Club would acquire an additional lease and yearly tenancy at a peppercorn rent from the Lord of the Manor (Onslow) of a part of the Common on which today's sixth, seventh and eighth holes lie.

embark upon the biggest budget project that he had ever worked on in Europe.

In December 1921, he outlined his plans for the New Course, which he hoped would be ready for sowing by August or September 1922, at a cost of £8,000 plus fees. It would be partially funded by Life Memberships at £150 each and partially funded by the issue of debt. An Extraordinary General Meeting was held on 17 December "to make the necessary additions and alterations in the Rules of the Club to give the Committee power to borrow the money required for the New Course".

Colt employed 30 year old J.S.F. (John Stanton Fleming) Morrison, who at the time lived with his mother in a house beside the 13th fairway of the (Old) course at Sunningdale, to oversee the work from an architectural perspective. An ex-Cambridge "triple blue" in cricket, football and golf, Morrison was a decorated war hero, one of the first Royal Flying Corps officers to have been awarded the Distinguished Flying Cross for gallantry. As well as being Captain of the amateur Corinthians team which beat Blackburn Rovers in the first round of the FA Cup in 1924, he would go on to win the Belgian Amateur in 1929 and the Sunningdale Foursomes with Joyce Wethered in 1928, 1935 and 1936. Henry Longhurst, his foursomes partner when playing for Charterhouse in the Halford Hewitt, described him as "massive, fit and fearless". Morrison's imposing and energetic presence on site was one factor which led to the New Course being ready for play by June 1923, earlier than planned and within budget.

Another factor in the speed of construction was the strong relationships that Colt had built with his contractors. The seeding was carried out by Colt's trusted agronomists Sutton and Sons, Turf Experts of Reading. The grass growth achieved through the autumn of 1922 and following spring resulted in Sutton and Sons placing an advertisement in Bernard Darwin's 1924 booklet on Sunningdale to boast of the achievement of turning "the Sunningdale New Course from seed to turf in nine months" which "undoubtedly constitutes a record of its kind".

J.S.F. Morrison, Captain of the Corinthian FC, cigarette card 1920s.

The sandy heathland at Sunningdale shares many of the same characteristics as coastal links land. Fast draining acid soil is the perfect base for fine grasses, which in the summer create hard bouncing, fast running fairways and greens resembling the courses of the Scottish coastline. Undoubtedly Suttons' task was made easier by the fact that this acid heathland soil had for centuries been enriched with the nitrogen, phosphorous and potassium of grazing animals.

Preliminary Levelling with Light Railway   *(SPORTS GROUND)*   *Preparation of Top Surface and Seeding*

Franks Harris Bros Ltd

GOLF COURSE CONSTRUCTORS

Experts in Landscape Work, Sports Grounds,
Playing Fields, Tennis Courts (Grass or Hard),
Croquet Lawns, Bowling Greens, etc.

Estate Development a speciality:
Comprising
Roads, Carriage Drives, Reservoirs, and
Earthwork of every description.

Important work has been effected on
over 100 of the principal Golf Courses
in the United Kingdom, including
the Eden, and New Course at St.
Andrews; the New Course at Walton
Heath; the Felixstowe Course;
R.A.C. Course at Epsom; also on
Links in France, Belgium and Spain.

Among others now under construction are
the New Courses at Addington, Sunningdale
and Moor Park, Rickmansworth.

Telegrams: "Franks, Station Approach, Guildford"
Telephone: No. 77 Guildford

STATION APPROACH, GUILDFORD

Claude Harris employed large gangs of labourers to construct new courses.

Sutton's Grass Seeds

FOR GOLF COURSES

PUTTING GREENS, TEES and the FAIRWAY

TURF ADVISORY DEPARTMENT.

For many years it has been a feature of our business to offer Golf Club Secretaries and Green Committees expert advice (either by personal visits or by correspondence) on the formation and upkeep of the finest golfing turf, and to assist in solving any special difficulties with which they may be faced. The value of the advice and assistance we have been able to render is indicated by the many appreciative letters sent to us from all parts of Great Britain as well as the Continent. The services of our expert advisory staff and the resources of many years' unique experience are at the disposal of every Golf Club in the country. Particulars as to terms on which special visits can be arranged may be obtained on application.

A VIEW OF THE NEW COURSE AT SUNNINGDALE
Showing constructional work in progress

The entire course was sown down by us in the month of August with seed mixture specially prescribed by our House.

SUTTON & SONS
TURF SPECIALISTS, READING

Sutton and Sons used horses to plough the land and sow seeds.

To build the course, Colt again contracted Messrs Franks, Harris Bros, the biggest and best professional golf course construction division in the country (now based in Sunningdale). Claude Harris explained one of the secrets of his company's success:

"One of the most important things of all is to find good foremen for the work. You see, we get the plan of the whole course, and the plan of each individual hole, as supplied by the designers. The foreman appointed goes down and gets his men together, and then the work is begun. The first part of the work is generally clearing hedges, trees, wood or heather, and often in doing a lot of necessary draining. Then

the foreman parcels out the work among his gang,
arranging as far as possible that all the men should
be near enough to him to be under his supervision.
I naturally have to leave a lot to my foreman, but
I get round to see him as often as possible, plan
out for him the shapes of the bunkers, and see that
in the formation of the greens and the contours of
the putting surface he is carrying out the original
designs. It really is wonderful how these foremen
fall into the general scheme of things. Now and then,
naturally, one will fail to appreciate what is wanted,
or the right way to go about it, but on the whole we
have been very lucky, and I would unhesitatingly
say that this firm owes a lot to the intelligent work
of the foremen that we have. Possibly, too, my
early training in landscape gardening has been of
some assistance to me, because you know Mr Colt
is very keen, not only that every hole should be a
good golfing hole, but that there should be a certain
picturesqueness about the whole course, as well as
about each individual hole."

Colt liked elevated greens because they were simultaneously
easy to identify but hard to approach: they restricted the
view of the flag for the second shot, making the golfer form
a judgement as to how far or hard the ball had to be hit.
The short second hole is a good example of this: the green is
32 yards deep but it is hard to know from the tee, even when

the ball has been struck well, exactly how far down the green the ball has travelled, because the slight elevation of the green hides the putting surface from view.

Writing about the second hole in an article about the construction of the New Course for the *Motor Owner* magazine in 1922, Charles Ambrose decided "the chief feature about it is the wonderful modelling of the green for which the contractor (Mr Claude Harris) inspired by Mr Colt, is entirely responsible; Dame Nature made it all dead flat an uninteresting, and has been severely improved upon."

But the first challenge that Colt had to overcome was how to fit two new fairways on the land leading up to the Clubhouse, in addition to the two fairways of the Old and the two belonging to the Nine Hole (finishing at the top of today's practice ground). Ambrose described the solution: "the old 18th green is to be shifted into the Clubhouse garden, where the flagstaff now stands, while the old first tee will be moved away towards the Club entrance".

The construction of the New Course therefore resulted in a significant change to the design of the 1st and 18th holes of the Old: no longer would these holes cross each other. In the process, space was made for a first tee for the New Course on the site of the former first tee of the Old Course, and for the 18th green of the New Course to be constructed below it and to its left from the perspective of the Clubhouse.

By today's standards, very little earth was moved for the construction of the New but, at the time, the *Field*

The approach to the New Course 18th green, under construction 1922. The 18th of the Old Course is seen to the left, just above the new first tee of the New; the first and ninth holes of the Nine Hole cover ground to the right.

magazine was critical of the amount of earth moving that had to be done to give the golfer a view of the challenges that lay ahead from the tee, as well as to build up the greens. Colt did not like blind shots and he would move as much earth as he possibly could on the New Course to ensure the golfer could see the ball finish. The only blind drive on the course was the sixth, which was played from today's ninth tee to a fairway which is now covered in heather and gorse, situated parallel but to the left of today's ninth fairway.

Colt liked fairways to be as wide as possible to create strategic options which forced golfers to think about how they are going to play each hole. Width, length and elevation were applied to particularly great effect on holes 6 to 10 of Colt's New Course, each tee shot asking a strategic question. Doglegs – another architectural device to get the golfer thinking – appeared on holes 3, 4, 7, 11, 12, 16 and 18. Colt is credited with having been the inventor of the dogleg.

The Nine Hole Chauffeurs Course, 1931, running around the houses on Titlarks Hill. The 15th green of the New Course is on the bottom right, the 16th tee just above it, and the 16th green on the far left of the photo. In the bottom middle sit the two fairway bunkers of the New Course third hole, below the dogleg 16th fairway. The 18th greens of the Old, New and Nine Hole courses are at the top left. Sitting above and marginally to the left of their respective 18th greens, the first tees of the New and the Nine Hole are also visible. Credit: Historic England.

A view of the open landscape from above the sixth tee. The tee shot was played from a spot forward of today's sixth tee leftwards to a high fairway running alongside the ridgeway path.

The New Course was largely devoid of trees when it was built (except at holes 7–9[16]), with heather, gorse, sand and rough waste ground providing penalties enough for the wayward hitter. While acknowledging that they were "undoubtedly charming features in a landscape view", Colt described trees in an *Essay on Golf Course Architecture* as "a fluky and obnoxious form of hazard," and trees were very rarely sited anywhere close to greens or fairways.

Colt's layouts would have natural undulations on fairways and on greens, but he did not believe in making the putting surface of greens too tricky. Most of his greens on the New

---

16 The old Colt loop of holes 7-9 were set in the woods to the right of the tenth of the Old Course. Play on these holes would be abandoned twice: first in 1935 and again in 1938.

Example of a Colt fairway bunker, blending with the topography and set at an angle to the line of play.

Course were shaped like upturned saucers, containing a relatively large flat area at their centre to catch the good iron shot; but running an off-line approach to the edges of the green and beyond. Run-off areas served the dual purpose of deterring both golf balls and rainwater. 'False fronts' which ran a weak shot back off the front of the green were a favourite Colt feature, and the New Course had its share of them (at 3, 4, 5, 6, 7, 9, 10, 12, 14, 16 and 18).

An essential feature of strategic golf is carefully sited bunkers. This course was being built before sand irons with large flanges (or 'bounce') on the bottom of the club had been invented, and bunkers were a significantly bigger challenge for the high handicapper than for the scratch player, so Colt did not aim to make bunkers too punitive. None of his

39

bunkers at Sunningdale were so steep that they needed to contain railway sleepers, rivetted faces or fat lips; they were styled to merge with the grass and heather that surrounded them, with a ragged sand line in order to soften them visually. Bunkers were cut in irregular shapes and placed where possible in the face of natural hillocks. Grass and heather tongues and noses would creep down the face of the bunker to make paths into the sand.

Before Colt, bunkers were often placed at right angles to the direction of play, but Colt positioned his bunkers asymmetrically. He liked to place bunkers across part of a fairway or in front of part of a green, making the golfer think about whether they wanted to take the risk of carrying the hazard, or of running the ball close to it, or if they would prefer to settle for steering well clear or laying up, leaving them further away from the hole but above ground. Colt's original holes 6, 13 and 18 (which all were replaced or modified in 1934) provided good examples of this.

His fairway bunkers almost always offered an element of risk and reward, and they were often set at different angles to the line of play, as can be seen in the case of the bunkers on the third fairway of the New Course and the (now abandoned) bunkers, the outline of which can still be seen today lining the fairway of the fourth. Colt bunkers set at angles on the New Course can also be found today on the right of the eleventh and twelfth fairways. Without trees to line so many of the fairways, Colt used wing-bunkering at the sides of fairways to provide a way-marker.

Horses constructing a wing bunker on the right of the fourth fairway, 1922. A group of men can be seen short of the green on the left hand side of the fairway.

Around the greens he tended to put in a series of smaller pot bunkers rather than large tracts of sand. The original (now abandoned) holes 6, 7 and 8 exemplified this, as do holes 10, 11 and 12 which remain largely intact.

What stood out for Bernard Darwin when the New Course opened was the strength of its short holes:

"In this respect it has certainly beaten its neighbour. There are five of them, the second, fifth, tenth, fourteenth and seventeenth – and all have charm and character... No architect has greater cunning than Mr Colt in producing the delightful glow of satisfaction in his patrons."

Colt would come to be universally recognised as the master of the short hole. When designing a course, he would often start

41

with the short holes and plot the longer holes around them. These holes, more than any, exemplify the Colt philosophy that a really good shot should be rewarded. The greens on these holes are smaller and are defended and framed by the natural contours of the land. Colt took the view that, because every golfer starts with a perfect lie from the tee on a short hole, they should find it easier to find the green and so bunkers on short holes could be placed closer to the putting surface.

Almost all the holes on the New Course that was built in 1922 have been modified in some way in the hundred years since, and five of those holes no longer exist, so the course that Colt designed must be described:

- The 492 yard scratch[17] 5 first hole consisted of an inviting tee shot, from a tee on a site at the top of today's chipping green, down the hill onto what is today's 18th fairway, before playing up to a small amphitheatre to the left of today's second tee, where the present 18th tee sits.
- The second, a 172 yard scratch 3, was the same hole as we play today, across heather to a long raised green.
- The third, a 401 yard scratch 5, was an attractive two shotter, played from today's forward tee.
- The fourth was a 438 yard scratch 5 played from one of two tees – one straight towards the green and the other

---

17 The individual 'scratch' scores for the course are listed on the 1923 card. A 'par' score, based on course length, was provided in relation to the whole course, rather than individual holes. No 'bogey' scores were published on the first card because bogey scores were calculated from the best average scores of first-class players over a particular course, and until the course had been played, bogey could not be assessed.

The fifth hole under construction, 1922.

from the right to an angled fairway – with way-marker bunkers to the left and a high bunker guarding the right of the fairway which, if carried offered the most direct route to the green (all these fairway bunkers were taken out of use in 1966 but are still visible in the heather today). A long second shot was uphill to a large green set into the side of the hill.

- The fifth was a 160 yard short hole played across a valley to a high plateau green. The green was guarded by a vast bunker stretching across the entire front of the green which had to be carried. The first teeing ground to be used for this hole was forward of the present tee.[18]
- The sixth was a 373 yard scratch four, stroke index one, played from the present ninth tee in the direction of the

18 John Whitfield (2000) believed that the shot was only played from the present ladies tee of the 13th after 1935 but photographic evidence from 1934 supports John Churchill's (2012) view that the tee was in use before then.

The second shot to the sixth green. A pushed drive would run right away down the hill to the right.

ridge to the left of today's ninth hole to a fairway over the horizon. According to Ambrose (1922) "The man who can play straight along the plateau will have a lovely second to play across a valley to the green" whereas Darwin (1924) describes "full horror which confronts us" in arriving over the brow of the hill to play the second shot. The green was cut some 60 yards to the left of today's ninth green, over the bridle path and above a steep bank of bunkers.

- The 377 yard scratch 4 seventh then turns left, facing south, into an area known as Longdown. According to Darwin, it "is a good hole too, with its drive from the highlands to the lowlands and then that nervous little pitch onto a narrow, sinuous green, set among the heather." The hole in 1923 was played from an elevated tee behind the sixth green to the right of the bridle path, although it was moved downhill to the left of the bridle path in 1929. The hole was a dog-leg to the right, with

The dog-leg seventh, over Longdown, 1922.

the second shot being hit up the hill to a sloping green cut into the side of the hill. The site of the green today can be found 30 yards short of a house in the wood at the end of a lane running north from the Chertsey Road.

- The eighth was a short scratch four of 324 yards with two sets of tees: one next to the seventh green and a back tee up a very steep hill to the right of the seventh green. The hole played downhill to a green that can be found today in the trees on the right hand side of the walk down from the tenth tee on the Old.

- The ninth went back up the hill, according to Stephen Sillem "to a saddle-back green on a col leading to the top of the high hill" over which is found the short tenth. Darwin described the hole as "very pretty with its second shot up a hill carrying a picturesque army of bunkers set *en echelon*". You can find the ninth tee today bisected by a

The eighth hole, a drive and pitch downhill, 1922. The white patch above marks the descent from the tee of the tenth hole on the Old Course.

gravel path running along the right hand side of the tenth on the Old Course.

- The tenth was a short hole played downhill to the same green as today but from a location above the then ninth green at a 45 degree angle to the left of the current tenth tee. Colt's bunkering design for this tee shot remains in place today.
- There then followed ginger beer refreshment at Battle's hut, located on the site of today's halfway hut.
- The 11th was a scratch five of 453 yards, a dog leg left over the same ground as today's 11th but to a larger and squarer green.

The tenth hole, postcard, 1920s. A downhill shot onto today's tenth green. Credit: Simon Haines.

- The 12th was a 302 yard two shotter played from today's forward tee, another good dog leg left over heather up to a high green.
- The 13th was a 560 yard three shotter played from an elevated tee, to a green 50 yards further on and to the right of the site of the present green, near the teeing ground of the short fourteenth. According to Darwin writing in 1924, only Mr Cyril Tolley (who had won the Amateur Championship in 1920 and the French Open that year) was capable of reaching the green in two.
- The 14th, a 189 yard scratch 3, was described by Darwin as "by common consent, I think... the best [short hole], with its narrow trough of a green that runs between bunkers on either side up to a little culminating plateau."

- The 15th was a dog leg as today with a ditch running across the entire fairway (there was no reservoir) at right angles to the bank which faces the tee and runs along the right hand side of the fairway. "The long hitter had a choice; to play the hole as a dog-leg, as intended by the architect, or to attempt to drive the ditch onto a relatively small landing area. A slight hook and he could be in trouble; he has to think, and weight the odds," wrote Whitfield. There was no bunker to the right of the green, enabling a low drawn second shot from an uphill lie.
- The 16th was a 388 yard two shotter played over the same ground as today but to a green sited immediately over the bunkers, 20 yards forward of the current green.
- The 17th was a 186 yard one shotter downhill to a banked green protected by fewer bunkers than confronted by today's golfer.
- The 18th, a 460 yard scratch five, was played up today's first fairway from a site forward and to the left of the then first green, close to the 18th tee of the Old Course. A good conventional tee shot thus landed on a fairway which cambered right to left, followed by a long second shot carry over a valley up to the green (on the site of today's first tee).

From left: C.H. Harris, F.P. Le Marchand and H.S. Colt, 1922.

With the New Course built, Bernard Darwin wrote:

> *"Sunningdale now has a network of courses, worthy*
> *of the East Lothian. On the one side of the road is*
> *the very charming short course of the Ladies' Club:*
> *on the other is the old course and the new course*
> *and another nine holes into the bargain... The new*
> *course may be said to take the high road and the*
> *old the low, so that, if this amount of comparison is*
> *not odious, the new is somewhat the more airy and*
> *open of the two and has from its highest point one*
> *of the most glorious of imaginable views – the Hog's*
> *Back, the Crystal Palace and I know not what other*
> *land marks."*

The New Course was officially opened on 10 November 1923. It measured 6318 yards, with an overall Par of 73 and Scratch of 74. At the end of the year, Mr H.S. Colt was nominated to become Sunningdale's Captain for 1924.

CHAPTER 4

First Alterations

One of the endearing features of Sunningdale as a club is that members are not afraid to express their opinions. While the Managing Director today responds personally to members who send in questions and views by email, for the entire twentieth century, the club operated an open Suggestions Book in which members would write requests by hand, against which members agreeing with a suggestion could write their name to indicate support.

In 1926, a Suggestion was made that "a slight shallow grassy hollow be constructed beyond the pin at the fourth hole so that a ball played up too hard to the green cannot roll back down the slope to near the hole thus converting a bad shot into a lucky fluke". F.P. Le Marchand indicated that the suggestion would be considered by the Green Committee. A very shallow grassy hollow is today discernible at the back of the fourth green which prevents overhit shots from rolling back onto the green.

The Suggestions Book shows us that, in the four years after the opening of the New Course, more and more members playing the first and 18th holes became frustrated at the presence of golfers playing on the same fairway in opposite directions. The problem with the tee as sited (in front and to the left of the first green looking back towards the clubhouse) was that there was nothing to stop tee shots from being hit left down what was then the first fairway (today's 18th fairway), with no obstacles preventing a second shot into the 18th green from there. Playing the hole this way inevitably led to some interference with players coming down the first. After much deliberation, the Committee decided on 25 June 1927 to change the fairways down which the first and 18th holes would be played.

The plan was to move the first tee to a site "to the east of the 18th green just below the eastern bunker guarding the green". From now on, the first tee shot would be hit into the face of the hill. The second shot would then be played across to the right towards the high first green which remained in place. On the way home, the tee shot at the 18th hole would now be played straight back up the hill, as it is today, rather than across the hill to the right. To enable a second shot to continue to be played up to the left, the 18th fairway was extended by 30 yards from where a short pitch shot could be played. The long hitting "tigers" could access the green with their second shot by hitting from the left hand fairway, rightwards over the bushes.

But the Committee had second thoughts about this scheme. On 15 October 1927, the minutes record that "it was decided to revert to the usual teeing grounds". The inviting first tee shot, a hallmark of a typical Colt course which eases players of all standards into the round, would for now be retained. A 1931

View from the back of the first green, from a postcard, 1923. The eighteenth tee shot is played across the approach to the first green to the right of the clump of trees, leaving an uphill second shot to the green. The first and eighteenth holes were laid out this way until 1934. Credit: Kevin Diss.

aerial photo[19] confirms that the original 18th green, guarded by three bunkers, did indeed continue in use; and that the first and last holes were also being played from the original teeing grounds. It would be another eight years before the issue of golfers playing from the same fairway in opposite directions would be resolved.

In 1928, the Committee received a letter of offer from Mr Tom Simpson, a Surrey-based golf course architect, who

---

19 See image *The Nine Hole Chauffeurs Course*, 1931.

Heart Attack Hill: Colt's picturesque ninth demanded a second shot carried over bunkers to a high green just below the ridgeline.

at that time was working in partnership with Messrs Herbert Fowler, J.F. Abercromby and Arthur Croome. He suggested that he should build a nine-hole putting course near the clubhouse for the use of Members, for which he would charge the sum of £900. It was decided not to have one made.

The Committee was more interested in addressing some of the concerns being expressed about the holes six, seven, eight, nine and ten of the New Course, which were regarded by many members to contain excessive undulations. Even with the plentiful supply of caddies to carry clubs, members disliked the effort involved and one of the holes (the 375 yard ninth) was known as Heart Attack Hill on account of it being uphill all the way to its high green. This was before the days of motorised trolleys and, after 1929, golfers were transitioning from having seven or eight hickory shafted clubs in the bag to fourteen heavier steel shafted clubs. A shortage of fit young men since the Great War meant that gaps in the caddy ranks were filled by young women and older men.

A subcommittee was formed in July 1929 to "investigate suggestions for alterations". In September, the club Committee took the decision to consult the members by means of a postcard, asking whether members approved in principle of the replacement of holes 6, 7, 8, 9 and 10 at a cost of at least £5,000. Those in favour of alterations numbered 143 while those against numbered 300, with 62 providing neutral replies. No further action was taken.

In November 1929, the Green Committee's recommended changes to the third hole were accepted:

> Bring the fairway up to 170 yards from the back tee and remodel the bunker on the left.

> Fill up two large hollows on the green, and raise the bank of the ditch behind the green.

A month later, further modifications to the New Course were sanctioned by the Committee:

> 2nd hole. Remodel the right hand side of the green.

> 3rd hole. Make a grassy hollow on the right hand side of the green.

> 6th hole. Make a new green at the bottom right hand corner of the fairway.

> 7th hole. Make a new teeing ground from the
> ridge short of the road and prepare a new
> fairway for the tee shot.

The new sixth green was built on a site short of today's
ninth green, before crossing the bridle path, removing the
formidable long and high shot demanded by Colt to his
elevated green on the hill to the left. A significant amount of
climbing would in future be avoided. And the change would
make the sixth much easier to play.

1929 saw the legalisation by the R&A of steel shafts for the
first time in the British Isles, after the Prince of Wales bought
a set from America and escaped a penalty for using them
in an R&A competition at St Andrews. Over these years,
innovative manufacturers were able to get the ball to travel
over ever longer distances, and the Standard Scratch Score
(S.S.S.) of courses all over the country had to be lowered. In
response to a request for information about the new S.S.S.'s
at Sunningdale, the Club Secretary F.P. Le Marchand wrote
in 1933 to Cap R.N. Dawes Smith of the Surrey County
Golf Union:

> My Committee feels strongly that the question
> of the handicapping of their members is
> essentially a domestic question, but if you
> particularly want the various particulars in
> connection with the Courses for which you ask
> we will let you have them.

In the case of the New Course, the S.S.S. was cut from 77 to 74. F.P. Le Marchand died within weeks of writing the letter.

The Club Captain that year was J.S.F. Morrison, who had been Colt's assistant supervising the construction of the original New Course in 1923. Since 1928, Morrison had been a full partner, alongside Colt and Alison, of their joint golf architectural practice.

On 27 October 1932, the Green Committee's proposal to build a new thirteenth green "nearer the road from where the present green begins" had been accepted by the Committee.

Harry Colt (left), John Morrison (centre) and Hugh Alison (right), 1928. Morrison was Sunningdale's Captain in 1933.

A year later, the Committee (that Morrison chaired) decided to leave the matter of the bunkering of the new green in the hands of the Green Committee. A further change to the New was also sanctioned: in July 1933, it was decided that the face of the bank on the left of the fairway of the 11th was to be made into a bunker. The plan was for all the works to be carried out later in the year, when a new Secretary had been appointed.

On 12 September 1933, Morrison convened a Committee Meeting in Derby House, London (home of the Earl of Derby) to decide who would take over as Club Secretary. One leading candidate was C.K. (Ken) Cotton, a Cambridge-educated scratch golfer and former schoolmaster who had gone on to become Club Secretary at Parkstone and Stoke Poges; he was a great friend of course architect Tom Simpson (and after the war would follow him into course design). Another was Major G.G.M. (Guy) Bennett, an Oxford cricket blue who played off plus two, represented Harrow in the Halford Hewitt, had been Secretary of Sandy Lodge Golf Club since 1920 and had been Hertfordshire Champion in 1928. Bennett was chosen by five votes to four over Cotton.

The Green Committee waited until Morrison had finished his term as Captain before decisively addressing the increasing objections to the mountainous holes six to ten.

CHAPTER 5

Simpson's Jubilee

In the 1930s, many of the country's old courses were being upgraded to take account of the length that the ball was travelling, not just because of the legalisation by the R&A of steel shafts in 1929, but also because of improvements to ball technology and the impact of mechanisation on drainage and the cutting of fairways and greens. One man who was frequently consulted on course upgrades was Tom Simpson, a flamboyant designer who had established his reputation in France, where he laid out the nine hole Valiere course at Morfontaine in 1913, extended the nine hole Fontainebleu course to an 18 hole layout in 1919 and revised Chantilly (Old) in 1927.

Tom Simpson gained his reputation in France.

Inspired by a debate in the bar at Woking Golf Club in 1902 over the placement of a bunker in the middle of the

fairway of the fourth hole[20] by John Low and Stuart Paton,
Simpson was a devotee of the principles of strategic golf design.
From 1910, he had worked as apprentice to Herbert Fowler,
subsequently going into partnership in the 1920s with Fowler,
Abercromby and Croome, all leading architects of that period
known as the Golden Age of golf course design – and major
competitors to Colt, Alison and Mackenzie. In 1931, he left the
partnership and formed his own company, Simpson and Co.

Although both were Cambridge-educated lawyers, Colt
and Simpson were contrasting characters. Colt was an
unassuming, modest gentleman, the youngest of six children.
He was steeped in collegiate and committee working, from
his Captaincy of the Cambridge University team in 1890 to
his participation on the R&A's first Rules of Golf Committee
with his friend John Low in 1896, to his collaborative work
with Alistair Mackenzie, George Crump, Donald Ross,
A.W. Tillinghast and many others both before and after
the Great War.

Colt built his fortune from very modest means and his
lifestyle remained modest throughout his life: according to
one resident of East Hendred, the village in which he lived
from 1915, Mrs Colt[21] "couldn't bear spending" and their
diet consisted mainly of vegetable soups from the garden.

---

20 Woking's fourth hole imitated the layout of the sixteenth hole on the Old Course at
    St Andrews, with a railway line marking the bounds of the course on the right and the new
    bunker placed in the middle of the fairway in a similar spot to the Principal's Nose bunker
    at St Andrews, tempting a drive into the narrow channel on the right side of the fairway.
21 Charlotte Laura Dewar (from the famous Scotch whisky family) married Colt in 1894.

Charles Ambrose described the personality of "the real Mr Colt. Quiet, unobtrusive, self-possessed, modest and even shy, but resolute as a rock. Seldom does he permit himself to make a gesture, and he never raises his voice. But the sooner you realise he is not a man to be played with the better you will get on. Technically, he knows his business as well as he knows his own mind, and in these qualities lies his strength."

Simpson, on the other hand, was the only son of a printing magnate, born into an opulent lifestyle. Although he expressed his admiration of Colt's work, which he believed had saved golf from the Dark Ages, Simpson was supremely confident of his superiority; he was widely regarded as opinionated and self-promoting.

Because Simpson was a man of considerable financial means, he was never reliant on golf to earn a living. This enabled him to be brutally frank in giving his opinions. Henry Longhurst described Simpson as "controversial" character who "didn't give a damn for anyone, particularly golf club committees". In the flyleaf to his *Golf Architects Bible*, Simpson stated: "Ninety per cent of the criticisms made by club members are due to Invincible Ignorance."

Donald Steel described Simpson as "a man of rich and varied talents, a distinguished golf course architect never afraid to speak his mind. It was a combination which made him a colourful and controversial figure, although his controversial side, coupled with a whiff of eccentricity, was the offshoot of a penchant for the spotlight".

Architects of the Golden Age: Tom Simpson, seated, with his partner and mentor Herbert Fowler. Sketch by Charles Napier Ambrose (1876–1946).

Simpson was certainly a showy individual (once driving his silver Rolls Royce slowly up and down in front of a club committee's window as they deliberated whether to accept his design) and vain enough to ask for a copy of his obituary before he died (Henry Longhurst sold him fifty copies).

Colt's professional rivalry with Simpson went back to 1921 over the design for the Harborne Golf Club in Birmingham.

On that occasion, Colt had first been invited to submit proposals but withdrew his plan in objection to the Harborne Golf Club asking Herbert Fowler and Simpson to visit the site and produce their own plan. In the event, the Committee decided that the Fowler and Simpson plan was 'unplayable' and implored Colt to take back control of the project.

Simpson remodelled New Zealand golf course with Philip Mackenzie Ross in 1931. A year later, he was commissioned to change Rye (Colt's earliest golf course design) substantially, building three completely new holes there (the first, third and ninth). By 1934, Simpson was busy finishing changes to Porthcawl, and the following year he made substantial changes to Muirfield and to Prestwick. Fred Hawtree wrote of him:

> *"Simpson was the ideal man for the role of classic thinker when so many mature golf courses felt the need for a facelift. He was aware of the risks of pursuing only length and slickness. As the older layouts from the mid nineteenth century seemed to run out of steam, he seemed to arrive at the height of his powers."*

Even so, it must have caused some upset to Colt and Morrison, who had both given so much service to the Club, to learn that the Sunningdale Committee had turned in May 1934 to their main competitors, Simpson and Co, Golf Club Architects, for a report into the feasibility of abandoning the mountainous loop of holes six to ten on the

New, and making use of the flatter land had been acquired over the back of the fifth green.

While Simpson shared with Colt a belief in strategic golf, the distance that the ball was now travelling led Simpson to the view that courses now needed to be radically altered – and made much tougher for long hitters. In his report for Sunningdale, he expressed the view that the Old Course at St Andrews was the "only real golf course", going on to criticise the way Princes had been extended to over 7,000 yards but still failed to prevent scores under 70 in the Open Championship of 1932 (won by Gene Sarazen).

To create a proper test for the long and accurate hitter who was now carrying ten accurately graded irons with steel shafts, Simpson was determined to markedly change the character of the golf courses on which he was commissioned to work. He wrote in his report on revisions to the New Course at Sunningdale that "the proper function of the first fairway hazard is to govern the play of the hole and to trap the scratch golfer's good shot, which is not quite good enough... The first fairway bunker or hazard should be so placed that it is not more than a few yards off the scratch golfer's most favourable line to the hole." Wing bunkers were not needed to trap the scratch golfer's good shot because they rarely hit the ball that wide. "There is no necessity to bunker the wrong line to the hole if the green has been properly sited," wrote Simpson.

Golf, he wrote, should be "a game of real adventure as against an examination of stroke production" combining "a pleasant form of physical vigour with the problems of the chessboard... No tee shot can possibly be described as good if the proper place is to be in the centre of the fairway... the vital thing about a hole is that it should be more difficult than it looks or look more difficult than it is. It must never be what it looks."

Many golfers today would take the view that a course should be set up to be fair, by producing results that reflect the quality of the strokes made. But Simpson wanted golf to be a mental as well as a physical challenge. He believed that a golf course should occasionally produce outcomes which feel *unfair* because golf is as much a test of character as a test of ability – more a reflection of life itself rather than of pure physical sporting ability. He defined a good golf course as:

> *"One that is laid out either on Links Land or Heath Land, and provides entertainment and a test of golf for every class of player, so that each hole presents one problem to the good player and quite another, a less exacting one, to the long handicap man. Finally, one which, from its very nature, works on the sub-conscious mind of the player."*

In *The Game of Golf,* Simpson explained that a golf course should make maximum use of the contours provided by nature; it should demand "mental agility"; it should allow for an element of luck; it should not be long for length's sake.

Simpson believed that a course which had variety would stimulate the imagination and encourage clever play. A course, he wrote, should ideally have as much triangulation as possible so that no two consecutive holes are played with or against the same wind.Parallel fairways should be avoided. Artificial construction work should be minimised. Every advantage should be taken of "the most striking natural features of the ground." Holes should be designed so that their challenges are visible, forcing the golfer to think about them. Par fours should provide an alternative route to the green for the weaker player, but they should tempt the scratch player to take a risk to get home in two.

These principles of strategic golf course design were first espoused by Colt, but they were enthusiastically reworked by Simpson as he tried to make courses tougher, without making them significantly longer. He was so determined to place dilemmas into the mind of the golfer – whether playing from the tee, fairway or on the putting surface – that differences emerged between his and Colt's respective architectural styles, notably over approach shots, bunkering and the character of greens.

How approach shots should be treated was perhaps the most marked difference in the views of the two architects. In his *Essays on Golf-Course Architecture*, Colt stated that:

> *"The consistency of the turf should be such that*
> *there is practically no danger of the ball being*
> *kicked to one side, or of being unexpectedly pulled*

up or shot forward. Whether the approach shot
be good, bad, or indifferent, it should receive the
treatment which it deserves and should obtain
the amount of run which its trajectory and spin
indicate. There are few things more irritating than
to find a patch of patchy and treacherous turf at the
entrance to the green."

Simpson, on the other hand, in his *Architectural Side of Golf*
declared that "A golf course should never pretend to be, nor
is it intended to be, an infallible tribunal" played according
to "principles of absolute and relentless justice." Simpson
believed in the old spirit of golf, where "luck" was regarded as
part of the legitimate fun of the game and where ingenuity in
overcoming unexpected situations was the real test.

Colt and Simpson also differed over the number of
bunkers needed on fairways. Colt regarded bunkers as the
most preferable of all the artificial hazards. He placed them
liberally on fairways, both strategically to introduce an
element of risk into the game (to tempt daring shots from the
tee to reach a more advantageous piece of fairway or to tempt
a strong hitter to make a carry onto the green) and as way
markers. Colt liked bunkers because – unlike gorse, heather,
water and rough grass – they required skill rather than brute
force to get out of. Wing bunkers had the added advantage of
preventing slow play because they stopped misdirected golf
balls ending up on other fairways or getting lost at the sides
of the course.

Conversely, Simpson tended to use bunkers sparingly and only for strategic effect. Too many bunkers, he felt, gave too much of an advantage to the stronger player. If "you supply him with a belt of clearly defined bunkers leading to the green, opening up the passage, he sees precisely what he has to do without further thought. With an iron club of which he knows the effectiveness to a few yards, and the assistance of a perfect method drilled into his system with which to back it up, the result is, as nearly as may be, a foregone conclusion."

Simpson wanted to make the good golfer keep asking himself "How far is it?" If all he sees between him and the green is open space, it would be harder for the good player to visualise the distance and trajectory of the shot that needed to be struck. On longer holes, he would often hide away the bottom of the flag behind folds of ground on or short of the green, so that distance judgement became even harder. While Colt used this tactic himself, Simpson used it much more frequently and mischievously.

On putting greens, Colt subscribed to what he called the "three essentials":

1. It should be possible to cut holes on 75 per cent of the surface of the green.

2. The ball should never gain momentum after leaving the club.

3. In holing out from a distance of 3ft 6in it should never be necessary to aim outside the circumference of the hole.

He followed that formula on his New Course at Sunningdale. Simpson acknowledged these general rules, and also agreed with Colt that a green should never be so difficult that it prevented a player from getting dead with his initial putt. But he made his greens much trickier. He wanted every green on a course to be different; he liked designing some greens with two levels and was comfortable designing large greens containing any number of mounds and slopes. All these innovations would, to Simpson's mind, help make the redesigned New Course a much sterner mental test.

On 27 May 1934, it was reported to the Sunningdale Committee that: "Mr Tom Simpson had paid two visits to the course and had submitted his suggestions, with some plans, and estimates for carrying out the work". The Committee was unanimously in favour of accepting Mr Simpson's scheme and resolved that an EGM of the Club be called on 9 June 1934.

On the evening of Saturday 9th June, an EGM took place to consider a resolution to approve Simpson's plans. The Captain explained that "the sum required for the whole scheme would be in the neighbourhood of £7,500"[22], that "we are hoping to give him quite a lot of credit for carrying out the work somewhat below that figure", and that "in so far as finance is concerned you can safely leave this in the hands of the committee". The club had sufficient monies in hand and income in prospect that no bonds were needed to be issued to

---

22 The work was to cost £7,748.

pay for the work. The Captain supported Mr Simpson's view that "if we carry out in its entirety the work indicated, we shall have the finest course in the United Kingdom".

The EGM approved Tom Simpson's proposals unanimously that Saturday evening and work began the following Monday. Simpson was complimentary about the way in which the New Course had been looked after, but he now had a mandate to build a radically different golf course which he alone would model[23]. The ground works, which involved a considerable amount of new drainage on the holes replacing the sixth to the tenth, were carried out by Claude Harris, who ran the Sunningdale-based civil engineering firm contracted by Colt to build the original New twelve years earlier.

It was to be named the Jubilee Course, in honour of King George V's Silver Jubilee of 1935. *Golf Illustrated* summarised the changes:

> "Nos 1 and 18 to be turned around, both with new greens.
>
> Nos 2&3 No change.
>
> No 4 New green on new site.
>
> No 5 No change.
>
> Nos 6, 7, 8, 9, 10 New holes on new ground.
>
> No 11 Completely re-designed.

---

23 There is no evidence that Colt and Morrison gave any assistance to Simpson as he implemented the changes but Morrison sat on the Club Committee which appointed him.

No 12 New green on new site.

No 13 Completely re-designed.

No 14 Minor alterations to green entrance.

No 15 New trees.

No 16 No change.

No 17 Minor alterations to green entrance."

The reversal of the first and 18th holes had been mooted but abandoned in 1927. Simpson now had the money to build two new greens and two new tees. He moved the 18th green to a position left of Colt's original green, further up the hill towards the 18th of the Old, located on the left of today's chipping green as you walk up the 18th hole. The 18th tee could be sited in the position of the original first green, making for a dead straight 18th hole up the hill, slightly shorter than the original 18th.

Simpson's reconstructed first green would be sited well to the left of the 18th tee, ensuring that golfers on the first and 18th did not get in each other's way. Simpson's first hole carries two of his hallmarks: the bunker some fifty yards short of the first green catches the slightly offline second shot; and the green complex makes use of the natural slopes of the ground. The new Simpson first green did not have the flat middle area that can often be found on Colt's greens. Instead, it tilted from left to right, and the ball ran off the back, front or right for those who could not land it accurately.

Simpson took out Colt's right hand cross bunker on the fairway 35 yards short of the green on the third, to make

distance harder to judge and to tempt a running shot into
the narrow entrance to the green guarded by bunkers. He also
took out "a protecting wall" at the back of the green on the left,
which had prevented balls going into a ditch.

The replacement of the fourth green was an attempt
by Simpson to reposition it on more natural ground to the
right of the elevated green that had been in use since 1923.
The second shot was no longer uphill and the ball would
no longer fall back off the artificial false front that Colt had
designed. Instead, like so many outward holes on the Old at
St Andrews, the flag could be accessed more easily from the
right side (which involved a riskier tee shot) than from the
left (which involved taking on the hump left behind by Colt's
old green). On many holes at St Andrews no part of the green
is visible, and Simpson's devotion to that Course resulted
in him attempting to recreate situations where the view of
the green was obscured and only half of the flag was visible.
Stephen Sillem described it as "a preposterous, tiny, hump-
backed green falling away in every direction which it was
quite impossible to hit from more than 20 yards".

From this point the fifth was exclusively played from the
teeing grounds which are today used for the forward tees of
the thirteenth. From this angle the uphill shot is played to a
flag on the horizon.[24] Shots such as these were a lot harder
without the distance measuring technology of today.

---

24 It was played from this tee until 1963, when it reverted to today's higher tee, which was
brought back a further 30 yards, providing a much better view of the green.

Colt in 1913, in front of the Sunningdale clubhouse, before leaving by boat to North America.
Credit: Simon Haines.

Route of the Nine Hole, 1911. Credit: Google Earth.

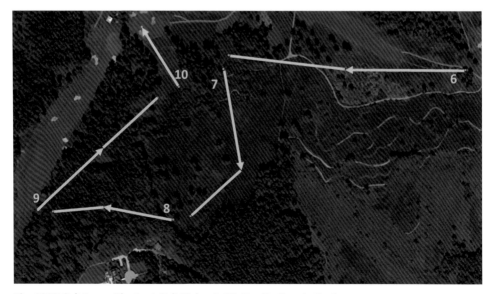

The 1923 Colt Loop. The Lost Colt Holes 6–10. Credit: Google Earth.

Views today from the disused tees of the old Colt loop holes 7 (above left), 9 (below left) and 10 (below right). Above right in the foreground is the site of the green of Colt's 8th hole. The tenth fairway of the the Old Course can be seen through the trees.

Layout of New Course Today. Credit: Google Earth.

Tom Simpson's 1935 Loop. Credit: Google Earth.

John Morrison's 1938 Loop. Credit: Google Earth.

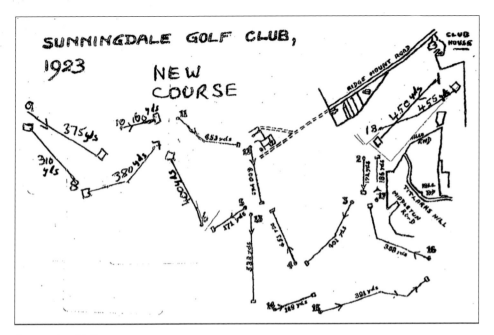

Course plan 1923.

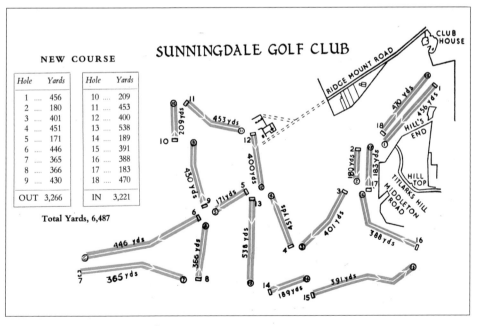

Sunningdale Golf Club, Official Handbook, by Robert Browning, Golf Clubs Association 1950.

Zarka's tree, situated between the third and fifteenth fairways. The Freeman maple is native to eastern North America.

In memory of
American Greenkeeper

ZARKA SMITH

Who died in a tragic
Motorcycle Accident
September 9th 1992

Zarka Smith's memorial plaque.

The next four holes of Simpson's Jubilee course were laid out on new ground over the back of the fifth green. They were constructed on the natural, wet heathland of the Common, underpinned by an elaborate system of drainage to ensure that fine grasses could grow on the acidic topsoil. On 22 September 1934, the committee approved Simpson's request for "insurance of the seed against a washout over a period of eight weeks from sowing". These holes covered the same ground as today's sixth to eighth holes, but they were played in the opposite (clockwise) direction.

The sixth tee was on a piece of flat ground to over the back left of the fifth green. The hole was a dogleg right, consisting of an attractive downhill drive and a short pitch to a green which today can be found 40 or so yards behind the large gorse bush that catches a hooked drive from today's eight tee. Back then the gorse bush did not exist; Simpson built a pot bunker on its site, forcing the drive to be hit left, thus creating the dogleg.

The seventh was a 170 yard par three from a tee which today would be found on the current eighth fairway. While the route from Simpson's tee to the green is today obscured by several trees, the long green that Simpson designed is the same seventh green that is played today. With this angle of play, the green would have appeared wide but would have been relatively shallow, with four pot bunkers cut closely into the green.

The eighth went in the opposite direction of today's seventh, a 425 yard dogleg left from a tee to the left of the seventh green out over the ridgeline towards today's sixth fairway. The second then turned left away from the swampy ground up towards today's sixth green. Some longer hitters would try to cut off the corner and, owing to a heath fire which had burned away much of the punitive heather, would find a reasonable lie on the bare hilltop.

Simpson's ninth tee can be found today in the heather looking back to today's sixth tee from the left of today's sixth green. The drive demanded a carry over the swampy ground down to the fairway, before a second shot up the hill (beyond today's ladies sixth tee) to a green sited ten yards short and fifteen yards left of today's eighth green, set into the hill below and to the right of the fifth green.

The tenth hole was played from the Colt's old sixth tee (the ninth tee today), a blind tee shot over the same ridge and onto a fairway which kicks the ball forwards down a steep hill. Guy Bennett explains:

> *"It was designed as a three-shotter, the third shot played over the present ninth green to a now disused site over the brow in the middle of the eleventh fairway. The eleventh green was designed as it is at present and driven from a tee nearby, the hole being much shorter than at present. This tee can still be easily seen, though now overgrown."*

The 11th was a very gentle short dogleg down the hill which some longer hitters could reach from the tee. The shorter eleventh hole provided some relief after the long and treacherous Simpson tenth and was necessary for the routing

A GROUP OF SIX NEW HOLES

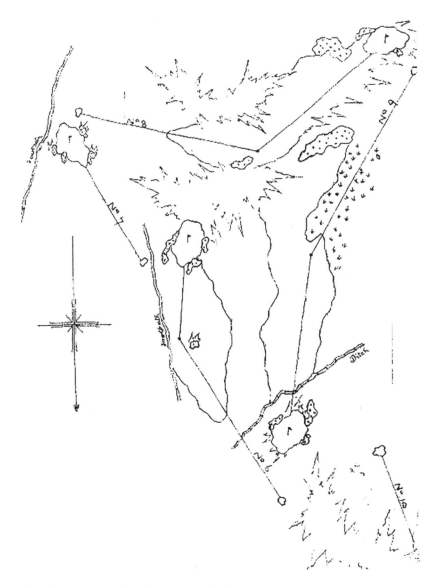

Tom Simpson's sketch of his plans for the holes over new ground.

of the course. But it no longer offered as much risk/reward as the shot from the 1923 tee designed by Colt near the original tenth green; and the new routing no longer brought golfers to the Halfway Hut, which was to upset much of the membership.

The 12th was remodelled by Simpson to create a sharper dogleg, with reward for those who could make a long carry over the heather with their tee shot, as they would be able to better access a small and humped green to the left of the green that Colt had built. Just as Simpson took away Colt's high green on the fourth, so he did on the twelfth, hiding the bottom of the flag in the hollow which today contains pine trees and scrub.

Simpson took every opportunity to make the golfer think. He shortened Colt's monster 600 yard 13th by over 100 yards, bringing the tee forward and building a new green on the left hand side, 60 yards shorter, to its current position. These changes turned the hole from a straight hole into a gentle dog leg. An angled set of three bunkers short and right of the green narrowed the approach. This was made all the narrower by the placing of a new bunker 30 yards short of the green on the left hand side of the fairway (the outline of which can be seen today in the heather).

The new green was sited on flat ground which Simpson thought would make the pitch shot a particularly hard one to judge (and time has proved him right). Simpson intended all his green complexes to be challenging, and true to form, the 13th remains one of the New Course's most difficult greens.

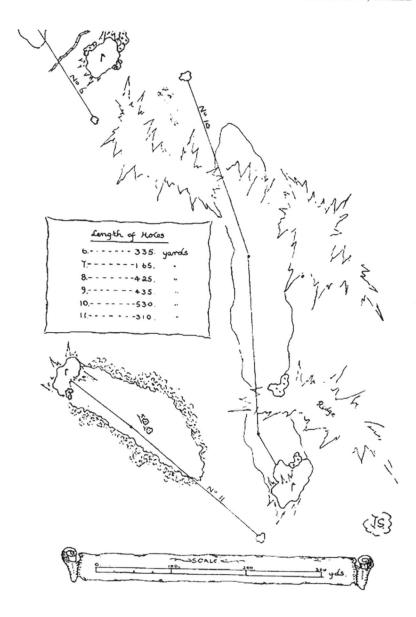

Length of Holes

6. . . . . 335. yards
7. - - - - - - -1 65. "
8. - - - - - - -4 25. "
9. - - - - - - - 4 35 "
10. - - - - - - -530. "
11.- - - - - - -310. "

Simpson's tenth consisted of a blind drive to the fairway. The third shot was played over a ridge to a low green.

85

The 13th is the most typical example of Tom Simpson golf design at Sunningdale today.

The short 14th saw changes too. The AGM in June had approved the filling in of the bunkers short of the green, which added little to the challenge of the hole. In September 1934, Simpson obtained the Committee's permission to extend the green and turn it into a double green, increasing the risk and reward of a shot to a pin placed on the higher level.

Simpson's Jubilee Course amounted to so much change that Henry Longhurst in the *Evening Standard* found himself making excuses for Colt's original design, explaining that he had been given a completely different set of stipulations by the Committee in 1922. In the intervening years, mechanisation had changed greenkeeping forever, with light tractors taking the place of horses to cut grass and sow seed and fertiliser. Holes no longer had to be close to the track from the stables at the back of the 12th tee and could be sited further afield.

Even so, changes this radical must have been hard for Colt to take. He was, after all, the man who had put Sunningdale on the golfing map as its first Secretary, who had turned the Old into the finest inland course in the country and who had created from scratch a New Course to rival it. Now his masterpiece had been all but torn up.

CHAPTER 6
Reversing Course

Soon after the Jubilee opened, a view began to spread among the membership that, in embracing Simpson's redesign, they had acted in haste. They were now repenting at their leisure. Not only was the Jubilee a very hard course to play, but it made for a less enchanting experience than playing on the neighbouring Old, and indeed than playing on Colt's original New.

As early as February 1935, just weeks after the work on the course had been completed, a Suggestion was made "that the cross bunker guarding the green at the third hole on the New Course should be put back," drawing a response from the Secretary that "the Committee are of the opinion that no further alterations should take place without a fair and lengthy trial." The previous course designer Harry Colt was not against cross bunkers and occasionally liked to force the golfer to play a pitch rather than a running shot; he had sited the cross bunker at the third hole forward of the green, creating dead ground between the bunker and the green. Tom Simpson had filled in the cross bunker, the outline of which can be seen in the fairway today.

In the year before construction began on Simpson's Jubilee, an extensive heath fire had reached right across the Common from the railway line, a part of it having almost reached the ninth green of the Old Course. Consequently, the whole Common was bare and black except for the new fairways and greens. As a result, the Jubilee Course was christened Abyssinia[25], a reference to the Italian-Ethiopian war. Former Secretary Guy Bennett believed "this appellation helped to damn the course and it was never popular."

There also remained substantial affection among a large body of members for the old Colt holes six to ten which, while undulating, provided a degree of protection from cold winds, as well as having the advantage of leading to the Halfway Hut. While the 1929 referendum had indicated that a substantial majority of members were in favour of keeping the holes, the mandate given to Simpson when designing the Jubilee was that they should be removed – and the June 1934 EGM had approved Simpson's plans unanimously.

On 21 November 1935 a Suggestion appeared in the Book "that the New Course as it was in Jan 1934 be maintained for play as well as the Jubilee Course". The Secretary replied that "This is being done for the present".

There were three good reasons why members wanted to continue play the old Colt holes. First, they were very good holes. Although undulating, the Colt sixth was one of

---

25 The *Daily Telegraph* report of the death of Claude Harris (22/6/42) referred to his "£8,000 new course at Sunningdale, known to some carping critics as 'Abyssinia'".

the most challenging holes on the course, the seventh over Longdown was a marvellous example of a short dogleg, the eighth a short downhill par four in an attractive dell, the ninth a good uphill challenge, and the short tenth gave a wonderful view from the top of the ridge down to a green surrounded by bunkering.

Second, being able to call in at the Halfway Hut[26] was reason enough for playing the old Colt loop. The new Jubilee tenth green and 11th tee were now some 250 yards away from the Halfway Hut, so few people playing the Simpson loop stopped for refreshment.

The third good reason for playing the Colt loop was that it was better protected from the elements. The holes were set in valleys either side of the ridgeline, and the old Colt holes seven to ten were tree lined which reduced the impact of the wind, whereas the new land that Simpson had used for the Jubilee six to ten was barren and exposed.

Just 18 months after the Secretary had given the assurance that the Colt holes would remain in play "for the time being", the holes fell into disrepair. A further entry into the Suggestion Book in April 1937, proposed by G.C. Cassells (who had left the Committee in March) and signed by 61 members, requested "that holes 7, 8, 9 and 10 of the New Course be brought back into play".

---

26 Also known as Battle's Hut.

On 2 May, the Committee instructed the Secretary Guy Bennett to respond, "The Committee does not approve of this suggestion," which sparked an angry response from Members on 8th May who found the Committee's response "most discourteous especially in view of the large number of signatures attributed, probably the largest number of signatures to any suggestion in the history of the club".

The Committee then gave the matter consideration and on 30th May 1937 stated that they "are now advised by the proposer that the intention of the original proposal was not, as appears on the face of it, that the 'old' new course should be resorted to in the face of a decision of the club in General Meeting, but that there should be facilities to play the old holes occasionally. The Committee see no objection to the proposal as thus modified, and effect will be given to it."

This response had the effect of appeasing the Membership and the old Colt loop was maintained for a while longer. In a further response in July 1937 the Secretary stated that the Committee had the matter "in hand", and it clearly took the view that changes needed to be made to the Jubilee so that the uneasy compromise could be resolved.

Having previously been Captain of the Club in 1933, J.S.F. Morrison rejoined the Sunningdale Committee in March 1937. In May the Committee approved three recommendations of the Green Committee:

1. That the new course 12th green be brought back into play at once

2. That a new 18th green be constructed as soon as opportunity offered, on the top of the hill, more or less on the site of the original Old Course 18th Green

3. That the Green Committee further propose to consider various alternative suggestions for certain improvements to the Jubilee Course, and subject to the approval of the Full Committee, submit the same to expert adviser.

In October 1937, the Committee approved the expenditure of £25 on an expert adviser, and J.S.F. Morrison was appointed in a professional capacity to submit a report to the Green Committee. His report was accepted and approved by the Committee in December that year, subject to the cost of alterations not exceeding £250 in addition to use of the Club's own labour. And so, just two years after the opening of Simpson's Jubilee course – which had torn up Colt's original design – Morrison and Colt were able to make radical alterations to the course that they had built 15 years earlier.

Rather than restore the original 1923 hilly and controversial holes six to ten, Morrison (with input from Colt) produced a new layout covering the same, flatter (Abyssinia) ground on which Simpson had built his new loop. Over the winter, spring and summer of 1938, the old Colt holes six to ten would be played, while Morrison got to work on reversing the Simpson loop, with the Committee deciding

John Morrison partnering Joyce Wethered in the Sunningdale Foursomes, which they won in 1936. He redesigned Simpson's Jubilee in 1938.

that "for the present these holes should continue to be kept in condition with the minimum amount of labour necessary".

Morrison's sixth was played from a low tee over the back of the fifth green, two straight shots alongside boggy land and drainage ditches to the right, with the burnt out land of "Abysinnia" to the left. It made use of the fairways that Simpson had built for his Jubilee course ninth holes and the green that he had built for the Jubilee course's eighth hole.

The seventh was designed on the land which had been Simpson's eighth hole, played in reverse so that it led to Simpson's old seventh green. A short par four downhill, the false front that Simpson created now sits on the left of the green, and any approach shot that is not hit with backspin will likely fall off to the left or run to the back.

The new eighth which Morrison and Colt designed was played as a dog leg left. The tee shot was played to the same fairway as today, almost blind in that a ball well struck can often be seen bouncing but not when it is rolling. The second shot was played up to a green on the left, short of the path which leads up to the next tee, on a site which today is covered in gorse.

Morrison's ninth was a shorter version of Simpson's tenth. The tee shot was played from the same tee (which had been Colt's original sixth hole) and followed the same blind route over the brow of the hill as the Simpson tenth. A well struck tee shot would roll to the bottom of the hill. While Simpson's tenth had been a three shotter to a green over the ridge, Morrison brought the green forward, setting it into the hill on a narrow plateau, and turning the hole into a long two shotter. The second shot would require both length and precision; anything that did not fly with backspin onto the putting surface would have to be run in from the left to avoid being kicked right away and below the green.

The final hole of the new Morrison and Colt loop, the par three tenth, was played to same the 10th green that had been used for Colt's 10th and which had been abandoned by Simpson. The green was surrounded by the same bunkers as in 1923, with the false front sitting now at a 45 degree angle to the left, on account of the original Colt 10th tee being 45 degrees left of the Morrison tee. By siting the Morrison tee on the other side of the hill from the ninth green, the walk from the ninth green to the 10th tee was reduced to no more than 50 yards.

Bringing Colt's 10th green back into play meant the eleventh tee could be pulled back to its original position, recreating the dogleg that Colt had designed. As importantly, making use of the original 10th green and 11th tees meant that the Halfway Hut was brought back within reach of players, caddies and dogs.

But the changes overseen by Morrison were not confined to reversing the Simpson loop. By restoring the 12th green to its former position on the plateau, Morrison added back onto the hole a treacherous pitch shot from the site of the Simpson green for those who missed the green to the left. Under the Morrison plans, variety to the elevations of greens was restored: the eleventh and twelfth greens were raised,

Morrison's remodelled tenth hole. From the Illustrated Sporting and Dramatic News, November 4, 1938.

Simpson's ground level thirteenth and double tier fourteenth greens were retained, while the approach shots to the fifteenth and sixteenth were to be hit up to natural plateaus, the sixteenth being a two tier green.

Morrison also turned his attention to the plateau green on the fourth. "Of the two-shot holes the fourth with its plateau green is beautiful, if one can play it as a two shot hole, which takes some hitting," had written Bernard Darwin in 1924. Simpson's idea of tucking the green away to a site to the right of the Colt green had proved unpopular. It was small, difficult to hit, with the bottom of the flagstick hidden, and

95

hard to putt on – all features that Simpson wanted, to make the course tougher. But it was visually unappealing and too difficult for the average member. Morrison moved the green back to its former, and current, position.

Morrison was asked by the Committee to move the eighteenth green "more or less" to the site of the original 18th Colt green, but the problem with that was that this was too close to the 1st tee of the New. Morrison's 18th green was instead sited backward and to the right of Simpson's; it is familiar to Sunningdale members today as the practice chipping green.

Morrison's changes were warmly received by Members and on 9 October 1938, the Committee resolved that "the new holes of the Jubilee course be opened for play as soon as possible and that a provisional scorecard and stroke table be printed."

At the 1939 AGM held on 11 June, a show of hands also gave a large majority in favour of Morrison's redesign, but the argument continued over whether the original Colt loop should remain open for play. The Committee decided, in view of the expense of maintaining the original holes as well as the new ones, to put the matter to a referendum. This gave a decisive result – 242 votes to 83 – in favour of abandoning the old Colt holes. They were never to be played again.

Is the 1938 Morrison loop that we play today a better loop than the old Colt loop of 1923? Until the site of those holes is again cleared of trees and scrub, the fairways resown and bunkers restored, we shall never be able to judge for

The fourth and twelfth greens, here seen under construction for Simpson's 1934 design, were moved back to their original plateau positions by Morrison in 1938. Credit: Historic England.

ourselves. But we do know that many Sunningdale members of the 1920s and 1930s very much enjoyed them.

The decision to bring in Tom Simpson to alter Harry Colt's original design for the New Course had led to six years of division and debate within the club. It had been driven by the fear that technology was changing the game so much that radical changes had to be made to the course. Many of Simpson's changes were made with the noble intention of preserving the spirit of the game and they did indeed set new golfing challenges, but tinkering with a Colt course is also a dangerous game.

Tom Simpson is today revered as one of the Golden Age's greatest course architects. His failure to win over the Members of Sunningdale is a blot on what is otherwise a deeply impressive architectural *resume*. Being asked to reverse the Simpson course must have felt to Morrison and Colt like a victory – and a vindication of their grand 1923 vision and project. We get an inkling of their rivalry with Simpson in a letter sent from Morrison to Hugh Alison in 1949, in which he wrote that he always thought Simpson was a bit mad, and having recently met him again, "he now appears to be completely bats".

In May 1951, the Committee voted to recommend Mr J.S.F. Morrison DFC for Honorary Life Membership "in recognition of the many services he has rendered to the Club both as Captain and in past years."

CHAPTER 7
War and Peace

As soon as the Declaration of War was made in September 1939, the Club was reduced to a state of general economy and run on a skeleton staff. Captain Guy Bennett MC resigned his post to rejoin the army and club member James Moir was co-opted as Honorary Secretary. New daily and annual green fees were set for serving military officers. Restrictions on the times that lady guests could play were removed. The Hon. Secretary was given authority to close the Nine Hole at his discretion.

In early 1940, the Artisans Section wrote to the club offering to maintain the whole of the Jubilee course, as it was still known, and the Club accepted their kind offer. That summer, the landlord, St John's College, agreed to reduce the rent to the club in return for the assurance that no part of the course would go derelict. In 1941, the Clubhouse was taken over by the War Office and a temporary Clubhouse was made out of the caddie enclosure. On 2 May 1942, the Committee took the decision to close the New Course for play but stated their intention to use "Every effort with the labour available... to preserve it as far as possible." The Old Course continued to be occasionally used, for casual golf, mainly by troops stationed at the nearby barracks.

Within a year, the New Course itself had been requisitioned by the Aldershot district for military training purposes. The course enjoyed very little course maintenance at all after it had been taken over by the Army. The head greenkeeper with whom Colt worked at Sunningdale was Hugh Maclean ('Mac', as he was affectionately known), who had been Willie Park Jr's foreman for the construction works in 1900 and who had retired in 1939, having overseen all the reformation and revision to the New over the first turbulent years of its existence. Mac was succeeded by his son Jim, whose job it would eventually be to supervise the restoration of the course. But the Club only had sufficient funds available to spend on the New to prevent complete disintegration.

As soon as the war was over, the Club Professional, Percy Boomer, was asked to put together an estimate to the District Claims Officer for the cost of reinstating the damage done to the New Course by military occupation. This amounted to £603.97, and six months later the Secretary was able to report to the Committee that the War Department had sent the club a cheque for £601:19/-, "in full settlement of the damage done".

On 1 January 1946, G.G. (George) Kirke took over as Secretary of a golf club which, like the rest of the country, was struggling to pay its way. The retiring Captain G.D. Fox optimistically told the AGM in April 1946 that the New Course could be back in play by the Autumn of that year. He was succeeded as Captain by the James Moir who as the

Honorary Secretary had given so much of his time to keeping the club operating over the period of the war. The Club could not afford more green staff and on 2 June, Moir's Committee decided to apply for six German prisoners of war to assist in the reconstruction of the New Course. Moir stayed on as Captain for two consecutive years to try to get the Club back onto a steadier financial footing. Before finishing as Captain in 1948, a further cheque was received to the value of £84:2/1d from the War Damage Commission.

Despite St John's College agreeing to first reduce, then waive, its rent, the club relied on the personal generosity of several prominent members to stay solvent. One of those was Alfred Cecil Critchley[27] CMG, CBE, DSO (a first World War Brigadier General turned entrepreneur, Portland Cement director, one-time Conservative MP and founder of the Greyhound Racing Association) who was at that time Director General of BOAC[28]. He joined the Committee in 1948 and led an initiative to draw on the help of the Artisans[29] section to work on the restoration of the New.

---

27 AC Critchley was a strong golfer who won the King William Medal and Silver Boomerang at St Andrews in 1932 and the French Amateur Championship in 1933. He had the good fortune to play in the first ever Masters Tournament at Augusta in 1934 as well as to qualify in the last hundred at the Open Championship at St Andrews in 1939. He married leading lady amateur Diana Fishwick and was the father of Bruce who would become a fine Walker Cup player, distinguished television commentator and famous Sunningdale member in his own right.

28 The British Overseas Airways Corporation (BOAC), the predecessor to British Airways, took possession of the Dormy House to run it as a training college and as part of the deal secured limited playing rights on the courses for its executives.

29 The Sunningdale Artisans had changed their name from Ridgemount Working Men's Club in 1928.

The Artisans, who already had the privilege of being able to allowed play from the first tee of the Old from 5.30pm, would now have unrestricted times on the New Course on weekdays and shared times with Members at weekends and bank holidays. The agreement relied on Sunningdale Golf Club reserving "the right to end the assignment, if not satisfied with the upkeep of the course".

Brigadier General A.C. Critchley: soldier, entrepreneur and good amateur golfer.

The club was running a huge overdraft and racking up bank charges. An EGM took place on 20 November 1949, at which resolutions were tabled to admit lady members, to issue debentures and to raise subscriptions – all essential in the Committee's view to put the club's finances on a sound basis but which caused a huge split in the membership of the Club and subsequently in the Committee. The one positive that came out of that meeting was that a vote also took place to complete the job on the New.

In a sign of confidence in the Club's future, the Captain received a letter from the St John's College Bursar informing him that the College Council had agreed to make a generous donation of £500 towards bringing the New back into commission, while expressing the College's hope that rent payments would resume from midsummer 1951. An update was given to Members by way of a letter on 23 March 1950, that "The necessary work on the New Course is proceeding and a further five holes will be opened for play not later than 15th May. It is anticipated that the entire New Course will be opened in early 1951." In the event, the whole New Course was made ready to play in October 1950.

A new Secretary Bernard Drew (who had spent the previous 20 years as Secretary at Deal) joined as the new Secretary of the Club on 1 August 1950. He would hold the post for the next decade.

In 1945, Colt had officially retired from the partnership with John Morrison and Hugh Alison. Alison moved to South Africa in 1947 and worked on several courses there before he died in Cape Town in 1952, leaving Morrison as Managing Director of Colt, Alison and Morrison.

On 21 November 1951, Harry Shapland Colt died, deaf and alone, at his home in East Hendred, Berks, aged 82. Sunningdale Golf Club sent a wreath to his funeral. No newspaper noticed the passing of probably the greatest ever golf course architect.

CHAPTER 8

Trees and Other Hazards

In a note written for the club in July 1985, Stephen Sillem, who played the New Course in the 1920s and 1930s, recalled that that "the New Course was always a more rugged and exacting course than the Old and that "the fairways and greens of the original New Course were always firmer and faster than those of the Old Course – indeed many of the original greens had that character of seaside greens – so fast and true they could be."

The course played like a links course because it was situated on an open tract of sandy heathland containing very few trees. During the early part of the twentieth century, large tracts of heather, with extensive areas of wet heath and open bog, dominated Chobham Common. There was little scrub and the only trees of any great size were at the Clump on Staple Hill and the Lone Pine to the south of the Beegarden. The Club gave generously on several occasions to the Chobham Clump Fund to preserve this group of pines which sat alone on the brow of a hill across the open links.

The view from above fifth tee, 1923. The Chobham Common clump of pines are the only trees visible. Forty years later, trees would line every fairway on the course.

While the Chobham Common part of the course contained very few trees, the old Colt holes 7–10 on the Longdown side of the ridge had been tree lined. After 1938, when these holes fell into disuse, the area of the old Colt loop became overgrown. The fairways of the original Colt eighth and ninth holes (to the right of the tenth fairway of the Old course) soon became part of a pine forest.

In the interwar years, wooded areas grew up either side of the tenth, eleventh and twelfth fairways, as did a line of fir trees separating part of the first and eighteenth fairways. The Club employed a specialist tree surgeon in 1930 who suggested clearing a number of smaller trees on the right hand side of the fourteenth hole, the left hand side of the twelfth, and also in the angle between the eleventh fairway and twelfth fairway. Further thinning was suggested right and left of the tenth hole. The Committee approved of these suggestions and was even

106

enthusiastic about the idea of using explosives to remove trees which encroached upon the courses!

Colt did not favour the siting of trees anywhere near the various lines down which a hole might be played, as they removed the golfer's strategic options. But he believed trees added to the attractive look of a golf course and he recommended that "where very few trees exist every effort should be made to retain them, and in every case the architect will note the quality of the timber with a view to retaining the finest specimens".

In 1939, twelve[30] of the eighteen holes of the New Course sat on open land, free of trees. Neither Colt nor Simpson recommended the planting of new lines of trees to demarcate holes; for them, heather, rough and sand were sufficient to provide fairway markers. Both Colt and Simpson liked wide fairways, to preserve the strategy of the game. While trees could make a hole visually appealing by framing its view, they had the potential to reduce the width of the hole as they grew inwards. By encroaching on potential lines of play, trees could cause the ball striker to see less of the challenge before them, to have fewer strategic options to consider and so have fewer dilemmas to face.

But in the decades that would follow, numerous new trees did appear. This was a development that was to alter the character of the New Course forever.

---

30 Holes 2–8 and 13–17.

Extensive tree growth across the New Course at first happened by accident. Rough animal grazing on the land, which resulted in no new saplings taking root, had begun to decline after 1914 and had almost completely ended by the time of the Second World War in 1939. Over the period of the war itself, the abandonment of all but the lightest touch course maintenance resulted in the unchecked growth of saplings and gorse across the course.

In the decades that were to follow, the tree growth happened by design. Successive Green Committees were to adopt a policy of positively encouraging tree growth along the sides of holes. So why did they defy the architects of the Golden Age and encourage the new tree growth? Ten factors can be identified:

- The first was a shortage of manpower. Even if the club authorities had wanted to stop the tree growth, it did not have the labour. It took five years to restore the New Course after the war, and that was down to the dedication of the Artisan Section.
- The second factor was the reliance by greenkeepers before the war on advanced mechanical cutting equipment which had removed the need for animal grazing. During the war, the course saw neither grazing animals nor mechanical cutting equipment.
- The third factor was the reluctance to burn vast tracts of heather to control growth. The scorched earth look was not popular and had earned the Jubilee Course the sobriquet of "Abysinnia".

- The fourth factor was psychological. The first wave of Dutch Elm disease had first arrived in 1927 and there was general public concern about the future of trees.
- The fifth was that the Old Course had already experienced some tree growth and Members liked the protection from the elements that this provided. They wanted the same on the New.
- The sixth factor was that trees are visually attractive. Members wanted to feel they were walking in a natural, aesthetically pleasing setting.
- The seventh factor was lack of scientific knowledge. Nobody was advising at that time just how damaging trees, their root structures and the wrong combination of tree species, were to heather growth and turf quality.
- The eighth factor was disease. Burrowing animals had long been part of the rulebook, but as the deadly myxomatosis virus arrived in the wild rabbit population in the 1950s, rabbits no longer foraged in the rough. Fir trees and other hardwoods were able to take hold and grow.
- The ninth factor was what Tom Simpson used to call the "invincible ignorance" of golf club committees. Not all Committee members understood that courses that were more open created more "mental dilemmas".
- The tenth factor was that, at the time, the trees were a long way from the line of play. Nobody was warning about how invasive they would become in the decades to follow. Green Committee members did not see the trees on the New Course as a particularly invasive or penal hazard.

While the main consequence for the scratch player from the spread of trees on the New Course has been to simplify the course by narrowing the corridors of play and so to remove strategic options and dilemmas, the consequence for the handicap player was more time spent punching shots out from the trees. The Suggestions Book contains plenty of evidence in the decades after the war of the growing annoyance of Members that rounds were becoming longer. We can only speculate as to whether the spread of trees and scrub meant players spent more time in them looking for their golf balls.

When the course re-opened for play in 1950, Robert Browning's course guide observed "a picturesque hillside of birch trees and gorse" beyond the fourth green, "a forest of young birch trees on the right to warn us to steer wide of the dog-leg corner" on the par five sixth, and a "pine-wood on the right" of the approach to ninth green. "This brings us into a tranquil corner of the woods, which fence us in for the first two holes of our homeward journey. The tenth gives us a dropping shot of 213 yards down an avenue of pines to a well-guarded plateau green… the woods are still on either side of us as we strike off the eleventh…The sixteenth is dog legged round an angle of the wood on the right… for the eighteenth once gain we drive downhill – with bunkers on our left and a clump of firs on the right."

In a note written by the Chairman of Green John Langley to the General Committee in January 1956, he states that "the Green Committee strongly favour the planting of some trees

The trees establishing themselves on the right of the 11th fairway, 1950.
Picture from Robert Browning's Course Guide.

on the new course, not only to make the new course more attractive to the eye, but also less exposed and bleak." The areas that the Green Committee had in mind for planting "are between the 4th and 13th, the 6th and 13th and the 8th and 13th on the New Course".

John Langley's replacement as Chair of the Green Committee in 1956 was G.H. (Gerald) Micklem. The son of a stockjobber who made a fortune trading oil and mining shares, Micklem enjoyed a privileged upbringing in Sevenoaks in Kent, playing at Wildernesse, before attending Winchester College and Oxford University, where he flunked his studies in Philosophy, Politics and Economics but won a golf Blue in 1930.

Robbed of his best golfing years by the war, in which he saw action across Europe and North Africa with the Grenadier Guards, he won the English Amateur in 1946 and played in four Walker Cup matches between 1947 and 1953.[31] Micklem joined Sunningdale in 1950 and, after his father died in May 1951, he received a considerable inheritance. He purchased a large Arts and Crafts house which backs onto the 16th hole of the New Course, Titlarks Hill House. He chose to retire as a partner of Cazenove in 1954 and, with no family commitments, settled into a life dedicated to golf.[32]

Gerald Micklem CBE.

At Micklem's first Green Committee meeting in the Chair, the minutes record "It was agreed owing to the many difficulties involved that it was not practicable to plant trees on the New Course". But this was not the end of the matter. In 1958, J.M. (Jack) van Zwanenberg, who had just left the Green Committee, made a Suggestion in the Book that, to protect golfers from bitter easterly winds on the Common, a few strategic trees should be grown on the New, as existed on the Old. The Secretary responded that the suggestion would be considered sympathetically.

---

31 GB&I lost all four of them and his only win was in the foursomes in 1953 at Kittansett playing with John Morgan (of Little Aston) who was regarded at that time by Bobby Jones as the best putter in the world.

32 GH Micklem was a selector for the England Boys Team between 1952 and 1984 and captained the Walker Cup team in 1957. Working with Raymond Oppenheimer (whose family owned the Temple Golf Club and who set up the Golf Foundation), Micklem "professionalised" the selection process for representative amateur events run by both the English Golf Union and the R&A, of which he became Captain in 1968.

Over the next decade, more wooded areas would appear to the right of the eighth, ninth and 12th fairways. Club members became so used to the windbreaks created by the newly treelined fairways that they often complained when trees, scrub and rough were cleared. In 1968, for example, a group of members stated that they were alarmed at the amount of clearance that had been done to the New Course, claiming that the character of holes 9, 14 and 16 had been altered.

Jack van Zwanenberg, who favoured the planting of new strategic trees.

"Are we to destroy natural growth that has taken years to mature?" they asked. Committee member J.K. (John) Tullis responded that "only scrub, brambles etc have been removed", that "there is a considerable amount of replanting scheduled" and "we will be grateful if members will reserve comment until the work is complete."

With trees lining the fairways, many of the way marker bunkers that Colt had established could now be abandoned. The bunkers on the adjacent thirteenth and fourth fairways provide good examples of this. The outlines of several of these original bunkers can be seen in the heather and in winter they sometimes fill with water. The outline of a large bunker set into the hill to catch a short, cut second shot on the fourth, can also be seen today.

Strategic bunkers were abandoned too. On the fourth, a high bunker which captured drives on the centre right of the fairway, and a column of bunkers which captured hooks and pulls to the left of the fairway, were overgrown in 1966. The outline of the bunker can be seen and, although it is too short to concern anyone using modern golf clubs today, no equivalent bunker has been placed further down the fairway in the intervening years. A drive which, both Colt and Simpson would have argued, forced the golfer to think strategically from the tee, can now be hit to the optimum part of the fairway without having to carry a bunker.

At a time of austerity for the club as well as the country, allowing some bunkers to become ordinary rough was a change that the Green Committee supported. In May 1955, they estimated that the upkeep of each bunker cost £10 a year and that a project to reduce the number of bunkers on a serious scale could eliminate up to 50 bunkers on both courses. However, they Committee took the view that only the bunkers which "are an annoyance to very high handicap players should be cut out, since that would make the Courses more pleasant and easy for such players without affecting the character or difficulty of the Courses for better players."

In the following years, the maintenance of many carefully identified bunkers was abandoned and nature was allowed to take its course. Even the short fifth hole green, an island in a sea of sand, saw a reduction in bunkering.

CHAPTER 9

Morrison Returns

In September 1951, the Committee received a report from contractors estimating the cost of changes to the New Course 18th green. This would have been the fourth location for the 18th green, after the 1923, 1934 and 1938 versions. The cost of moving the green, at £400, on this occasion was regarded as too prohibitive.

J.S.F. Morrison visited the New Course on several occasions in the Autumn of 1955, having been contracted by the Green Committee for the sum of 20 guineas to produce a report suggesting further modifications to improve the course.

The proposals in his report were subtle, inventive and ambitious. For the short holes, he expressed himself satisfied with his new tenth, recommended new back tees for holes two and 14, and suggested reducing the height of the mounds short of the 17th green to provide better visibility from the tee.

Morrison was not afraid to be self-critical and took aim at many of the holes in the loop that he himself had hastily redesigned in 1938. He noted that "It is very obvious that holes 6, 8 and 18 are far from satisfactory." The straight uphill par five sixth hole, he claimed, was:

*"a dull uninteresting hole for golfers of all
handicaps. After considering various and numerous
possibilities, I have come to the conclusion that the
best way to deal with this hole is to make an entirely
new green on the right of the fairway about 70 yards
short of the present green and to move the tees
further to the right, where they will provide shots at
a more interesting angle to the fairway and also a
fine view over the common towards Windlesham."*

The intention was that, by building a new sixth green, the
original green (which had originally been constructed by
Simpson in 1934 as the green for the eighth hole of the
Jubilee) could be used as the teeing ground for the seventh.
This was an idea that the Green Committee already
considered and approved, in May 1955, subject to the
necessary finance becoming available to make the alteration.

Morrison recommended extending the bunker on the
right hand side of the seventh green leftwards by six yards,
"giving the player, who does not place his tee shot on the left
portion of the fairway, a very difficult approach shot."

He described the green for the eighth hole as a "most
unsuitable site", said that it was not worth tinkering with the
present green, and recommended that a new long narrow
green be constructed. This "would start just to the left of the

present green and extend in the direction of the present back tee[33] to the 6th hole."

The ninth "is another hole with its green on an unsuitable site." To give the green more definition and "give the player some idea of what he is trying to do", he advised a three foot mound at the back of the green and a two foot mound short right of the entrance to the green.

Morrison criticised the thirteenth as being "rather plain" and suggested a new bunker be constructed on the left hand side of the fairway about 75 yards short of the green. This would create a strategic dilemma for the second shot: go right of the bunker and leave a third shot over the row of bunkers short right of the green; or try to fly the bunker, incurring the additional risk that anything tweaked left would result in the ball kicking further left into the heather.

Morrison did not hold back in his criticism of the 18th hole, which he regarded as the weakest on the course:

"I have always disliked this hole. It provides hardly a single really interesting shot whether played by a champion or a beginner and is certainly not a worthy finish to a club of the standing of Sunningdale.

A really good interesting finishing hole is a tremendous asset to any golf club. It is often the first

---

33 The back tee of the sixth at that time was the current forward men's yellow tee.

hole a player remembers when he returns to the club house and if it is not interesting he is inclined to forget the many good holes he has played before it.

After carefully considering the pros and cons of the numerous ways the 1st and 18th holes could be improved, I have come to the conclusion that the best scheme will be to leave the 1st hole as it is and to play a new 18th hole from a tee just west of the original 1st green to a new green situated between the Simpson 18th green and the present 18th green. There is an excellent site for a green here...

A new bunker on the left at about 200 yards from the tee would be required to discourage play in the direction of the present 18th tee on the Old Course. Golfers who play their tee shot safe to the right will be faced with second shots from a very difficult angle."

The Green Committee accepted Morrison's recommendations but not all were implemented. Some jobs could be done immediately by the club's own green staff. For example, the bunker to the right of the seventh green was extended; and the mounds near the ninth green were agreed to.

For the reconstruction of the 18th green, the Green Committee minutes record in June 1955 that three of its members (J.D.A. Langley, G.H. Micklem and D.R. Foster) had identified:

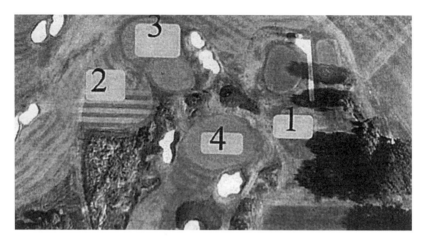

The four sites of the eighteenth green: 1=1923 Colt. 2=1934 Simpson. 3=1938 Morrison/Colt. 4=1957 Committee. Google Earth view. Green locations by John Churchill, 2012.

"an ideal site, which, in fact, was one of Simpson's greens[34], lying near to the forward tee on the first hole to the right of the present 18th fairway below the final slope up to the present green... The Committee would then suggest that the present 18th green becomes the practice green with practice bunkers around it."

However, in April 1957, the suggestion of using the old Simpson green was dropped. The plan was now that a new green would "be constructed to the right and below the

---

34 Former Sunningdale Captain and historian John Churchill has identified the site of Simpson's green to be short and left of the Morrison 1938 green, to the right of the 18th fairway of the Old Course.

119

present wore green." The matter of where to put the 18th green was finally settled.[35]

Each new green was estimated by Morrison to cost £500 per green and would need a bulldozer on site. In March 1957, the Green Committee recommended that the club should proceed with the construction of the new sixth green in addition to the new 18th, but took the view that Morrison's plan to improve the eighth green would not sufficiently improve the hole.

In addition, new tees would be built for the 18th, immediately west of the 17th green. It was acknowledged that moving the tees back this far would interfere with the 18th tee of the Old but that wire netting could be put in place to capture pulled duck hooked drives without detracting from the appearance of the holes. The minutes record: "When the new tee and green have been constructed John Morrison's suggestion of a long bunker to the left of the fairway about 180 yards from the tee will be considered." Over the winter of 1958–9, new bunkers to catch the hooked tee shot were put in.

A new "tiger tee" (today's white tee) was created for the sixth hole on the right, remaking the hole as a dogleg and providing magnificent views stretching across the North Downs; but the forward tees remained in place. A new green would be built on the sixth fairway below the original Simpson (eighth) green and it was agreed that bunkers would

---

35 More alterations were subsequently made to the green's surrounds in 1961, 1967 and in the early 2000s.

made from the natural hollows on either side. It was thought that making a pond from the cross rough on the right of the fairway, which was usually casual water, would enhance the look of the hole.

In April 1957, £1,200 was authorised by the General Committee to build new greens on the 18th and sixth holes. John Morrison's consulting services were retained for the period of their construction. In 1958, the Green Committee minutes record that Morrison put together a new plan for the sixth green, his last piece of work for the club.

J.S.F. Morrison died on 28 January 1961. His contributions to the development of the New Course are remarkable. He was there at the very beginning and exerted his influence over the setup of the New Course over four decades. Arguably, it has been shaped as much by him as by Colt himself.

CHAPTER 10

Cotton and Steel

Over the time he spent serving on the Committee at Sunningdale until his Captaincy in 1960, Gerald Micklem initiated significant changes to both the Old and New courses. One initiative was the construction of "tiger tees". In addition to the sixth and 18th, new back tees were constructed on the first, seventh, 11th, 13th and 15th holes of the New.

Micklem also suggested to the Committee that the first and 18th holes should be turned around, effectively back to the Colt design of 1923. This, he said, would not only improve them but would give an increased area for the Practice Ground after further clearance. After discussion, it was decided not to proceed for the time being. It was, however, an idea which did not go away.

With the changes to the sixth and eighteenth holes already in train, the question of where to move the eighth green remained open. Morrison had suggested building a new green below and to the left of the eighth green but this would entail losing the forward tees of the sixth. Another idea was to extend the green to the right behind a bunker, forcing a drive out to the left, which was also not considered satisfactory.

A new architect was hired to advise on the scheme: C.K. (Ken) Cotton. A brilliant scratch golfer, he was a former schoolmaster who then became club secretary at Hendon, Parkstone, Stoke Poges and Oxhey where Ted Ray was the professional. Twenty-seven years earlier, he had lost out on the job of Sunningdale Secretary to Major Guy Bennett.

Cotton was a great friend and follower of Tom Simpson, who bequeathed him a copy of the Simpson's hand-written 'Golf Architect's Bible' described by his friend and future business partner Donald Steel as "an amazing leather bound miscellany of architectural and greenkeeping 'secrets'". Cotton did not start working as a golf architect until he was 50 but he saw potential opportunities in reclaiming layouts that had been neglected or fallen into disrepair during World War II. Amongst the courses he worked to restore in the post-war era were Royal Lytham, Royal Porthcawl and Saunton Sands.[36]

In a fairly flat market for new golf courses, he was responsible for St Pierre and Cradoc in Wales, Ross-on-Wye in Gloucestershire, extending Frilford Heath from 27 to 36 holes, and a number of courses in Europe, the most famous of which was Olgiata in Rome. D.C.M (Donald) Steel later joined Cotton's architectural practice – Cotton (CK), Pennink, Lawrie and Partners – combining this work with his duties as golf correspondent for the *Sunday Telegraph*. He

---

36 CK Cotton was a founding member, Chairman and President of the British Association of Golf Course Architects. He designed the Green course at Frilford Heath and the short course at Wentworth as well as having numerous commissions in Europe.

described Ken Cotton as "my boss and a lovely man with a manner that won him friends everywhere.".[37]

Cotton was paid 25 guineas by the Club for a report into the eighth green. He suggested building a green some 30 yards to the right and 30 yards backward of the existing eighth green, below and to the right of the fifth green. This would take away the dogleg but it would demand a longer and more accurate second shot into

Ken Cotton.

the green. Any second shot landing short or right would be kicked away from the green to the bottom of the hill on which the green would be perched, while second shots that were overhit would leave similarly challenging chip shots from below the hole.

The Committee received his report in July 1960 and agreed to the scheme. Construction work began in September 1961 and the new green was ready for play the following spring. Minor modifications were made to it the following autumn, such as the extension of three yards of turf behind the green.

Ken Cotton visited the club again in October 1963 to produce a report on alterations to the fifth hole. He suggested

---

37 Interview with Donald Steel, 19 October 2023.

moving the fifth tee away from its "Simpson tee" which was sited at the bottom of the hill on the current forward thirteenth tee. The tee would be moved to the right, back to the "site of the old disused tee" which Colt had created in 1923. This made the tee shot visually more attractive but, arguably, easier to execute because players could see the whole green laid out before them.

He presented a further report in 1965, in which he made recommendations to put more heather on the fairway of the 17th; to level the left hand back quarter of the first green to provide more places for cutting the hole; to make the tiger tee on the sixth the medal tee; to build a brand new green on the 18th; to construct a new water hazard to the right of the 15th fairway; and a to put in a new bunker on the ridge to the right of the 15th green.

The plan for the 15th is a good example of a new philosophy of golf course design which emerged after the second world war. Some have called it "heroic school" of golf design, embodying the best principles of both the penal and strategic design schools. The advent of the mechanised digger meant that large man-made lakes and bunkers could now be constructed to create strategic choices. The stronger player who was prepared to take more risk from the tee could be rewarded with a heroic outcome by carrying the penal hazard.

The ditch which ran across the fifteenth fairway could be filled in and replaced by a pond, strategically positioned to catch the weak or sliced drive off the tee. The longer hitter could now carry the lake with their best drive and land on a section of the fairway where there was no longer a danger of catching the ditch.

Cotton's plan for a new 18th green was more radical:

"The hole should be made a right to left dog-leg with a new green just short of the 18th green of the Old Course. This would result in a very fine and testing second shot for the good players if they feel they were to reach the green, and it would become a real par 5 of (we judge) about 500 yards. For good players the present hole is not really a par 5, although under the SS Score system[38] it ranks as such.

The site we propose for the new green will be recognised by some of your more elderly members as that on which the original 18th green of the Old Course was built...

We would stress that, in our opinion the hole, if played to the new green, would make a very fine finish indeed to the course."

This new green would be sited just beyond Simpson's 1934 green. When the Green Committee met in December 1965, opinion was divided over the proposal. Cotton returned to

---

38 At the time the 18th was a par four, making the course par 69, but SSS 71.

the course in February 1966 and wrote in his second report that, while he recognised that there was a difference of opinion – some members maintaining that it would be too dangerous being sited so close to the 18th green of the Old Course – the green could be sited further to the right, in effect on the practice chipping green on two levels.

The proposal was not enacted. In July 1967, the new Chairman of the Green Committee, Nicholas Royds, held a committee meeting on the 18th green of the New and set out a plan of his own. His proposal was to increase the area of the green, with a sloping extension on the left hand side and deep bunker on the right. A small pot bunker would be built on the far side and to the left of the green. Work commenced on the Royds scheme that Autumn.

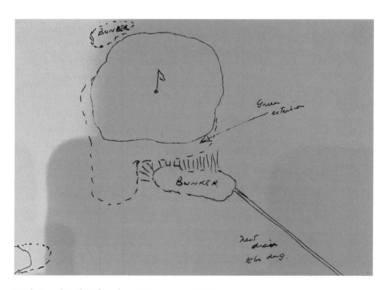

Nick Royds' plan for the 18th green, 1967.

The most significant change to the course in 1969 was the filling up of the ditch which ran from the pond diagonally across the fairway of the 15th, while the winter of 1970 saw a subtle change to toughen up the fifth hole: the removal of a bunker on right of the fifth green, which didn't drain properly, and its replacement with a bunker cut into the green on the right hand side.

It was at this time that, Donald Steel, who had been with Cotton (CK), Pennink and Lawrie since 1965, became a partner in the firm. He became the person to whom Sunningdale Golf Club would turn for architectural reviews over the next thirty years.

Donald Steel learned to play golf at Denham as a boy in the 1940s under the tutelage of John Sheridan, son of Sunningdale's Caddiemaster Tommy Sheridan. As a young man, he would often drive John Sheridan over to see his father and take the opportunity to play the Sunningdale courses. Steel qualified to play in the Open Championship at St Andrews in 1970, the same year in which he represented England in the Home Internationals at Royal Porthcawl and scored his second victory in the President's Putter at Rye. To this day, he takes the view that, to be a good golf course designer, it helps if you play the game too.

C.K. Cotton died shortly before his 87th birthday in 1974, bequeathing Tom Simpson's *Golf Architect's Bible* to Donald Steel. Their business partner (and Steel's Halford Hewitt partner from Fettes) Charles Lawrie died the following year aged just 53. Michael Bonallack also worked with Frank

Pennink and Donald Steel on some of the firm's commissions, before he was appointed R&A Secretary in 1983.

Donald Steel paid another visit to Sunningdale in October 1976. In his report, Steel suggested further changes to the finishing hole. Having considered the report the following February, the Committee deputed D.H.R. (Bugsy) Holland to mark out the position of a new bunker by the

Donald Steel.

18th green. The bunker on left of green was to be moved much nearer the putting surface.

Thinking back[39] over the reports that he prepared for Sunningdale's courses, Donald Steel endorsed Colt's advice that a course should not be changed too much. His emphasis was on "making adjustments rather than major change".

One adjustment that Steel recommended in his 1976 report was that a bunker be built to the right of the 8th green to catch the ball that otherwise kicked into rough, scrub or gorse at the foot of the hill. The Green Committee recommended the change, but it was not accepted by the General Committee and the bunker has never appeared.

---

39 October 2023 interview.

The eighth is unique in that it is the only hole on the New Course without a bunker.

In 1980, the eleventh tee was extended back nearer to the halfway hut. The following year, Steel paid another visit and suggested further modifications: the 14th medal tee should be moved back 30 yards and to the right of existing 14th tee to make the most of the water feature; the ditch on the tee side of the fairway would be extended to the pond; and the seventh tee should lifted and levelled to make the tee shot over the hill less blind. All the recommendations were adopted by the Green Committee, chaired at that time by C.R. Burn.

Over the following decade very few changes were made to the design of the New Course. Lawson Bingham joined as Course Manager in 1991. In his May report of that year to the Green Committee, he noted that:

Virtually all the ladies tees have far too long a carry to the fairway for the average lady player. My suggestion is that over the coming years we re-site on more forward positions, in consultation with lady members. The advantages being:-

A. *More space for the men on the current tees with red markers*
B. *Speed up play not looking for balls on the carry's*
C. *Peace and quiet at dinner for the husbands that are members.*

The Green Committee minutes from the following September record that the programme to re-site some of the ladies' tees will have to be delayed and fully discussed with the Captain before being implemented.[40]

A new championship back tee was built on the sixth hole in 1992, up the public footpath that leads to Longdown, way back to the right of the existing tee on the hill. The view of the North Downs is even more spectacular, while the section of fairway to aim at is reduced to the size of a postage stamp. The greenside bunker to the right and back of the sixth green was filled in the same year.

1997 and 1998 also saw the construction of new teeing grounds to accommodate blue championship tees. A new tee was built into the bank behind the par three tenth tee, for example, taking the tee shot to over 200 yards. A new blue tee on the fifteenth increased the length of the hole by a further 20 yards.

As Sunningdale Golf Club prepared for its centenary, Donald Steel was invited back by the Committee to review the courses. In January 2000, he made a presentation, in which he explained that indicated that changes were needed because of the dramatic change in equipment that had taken place over a relatively short period of time, because of the changes in woodland which had been allowed to happen, and

---

40 Sunningdale today is a subscriber to the R&A's Women in Golf Charter, a strong statement of intent to take measures designed to achieve positive change for women, girls and families.

because of the decline in the proportion of heather which had suffered through the reduction in light and the competition of the grasses.

Steel returned in May with his recommendations. For the New Course, he recommended that the seventh and eighth holes should be lengthened, with new championship tees built behind the existing tees. There was some support for this proposal in the Green Committee but permission would be required from English Nature, as the extended tees would fall on land which the Club owned but which was now designated as a Site of Special Scientific Interest (SSSI), and they did not believe the chances of obtaining permission to be high enough.

Another recommendation from Steel concerned the first and 18th holes. Like Colt, he took the view that the first hole on any course should consist of an inviting drive, one that would enable a group to get away quickly out onto the course. "Colt," said Steel "was not a cruel architect. He liked to give everybody a chance." What Sunningdale now had as its first hole on the New Course, according to Steel, was "a rather terrifying hole, where even a good drive leaves not remotely the easiest of lies, and then a long second shot to a green that is difficult to hit." He suggested that the first and 18th be switched around, so that they ran over the same ground that Colt had designed for them in 1923.

The redesigned first would consist of an inviting downhill tee shot and a second shot to an amphitheatre green below the second tee, while the eighteenth hole would consist of a dramatic second shot from the top of the hill over the valley to a high green on the hill below the car park. This was essentially the same proposal that Gerald Micklem had put to the Green Committee in 1960. Forty years later, the Green Committee again rejected this idea.

CHAPTER 11

Keeping the Greens

It was in 1965 when the club first took out an annual subscription entitling it to a visit every year from turf experts from the Sports Turf Research Institute. A visit took place in June of that year and a report was prepared, which was made available to all members of the club. The report noted that the quality of the turf on the New was of slightly better texture than the Old Course greens. The prescription for the greens involved keeping the cutters high early in the season, plus plenty of spiking, slitting and tining at appropriate times of the year. They report also said "We do not advise watering the fairways artificially since we think this would make the grass too lush and out of character with this golf course."

With the point about fairway watering taken on board, an estimate was received from "British Overhead Irrigation Ltd" for supplying and installing a fully automatic "pop up" sprinkle watering system for the greens, tees, green approaches on both courses and the putting green only. This came to £14,725. Sunningdale became the first club in the British Isles to introduce automatic watering in October 1966.

It was not long before green staff soon discovered that the clay subsurface of the greens was retaining too much water, encouraging the growth of meadow grasses on the greens. The greens on the New Course were constructed using the same dewpond method as for the Old, using a clay base to retain water within the soil above. In an era before automatic watering, it was the only way to ensure the greens stayed green. Never had Colt's words rung so true that "the plagues of Egypt seem but slight evils in comparison with the trials sometimes expressed by the keen and anxious greenkeeper."

The overwatering and over-fertilising of greens led to a problem never before experienced at Sunningdale: soft, pudding greens that frequently flooded. By the mid-1970s, the greens on both courses had lost many of their deep-rooted fine grasses and were now dominated by meadow grass. One solution to the appearance of so much *poa annua* was the boring of deep holes into the greens each year, to break up the clay subsurface and enable water and air to flow through to the roots and so encourage finer grass growth. Another solution was to water the greens less often.

The leading advocate of such methods was J.H. (Jim) Arthur. Born in Camberwell, south London, Arthur had read agriculture at Reading University before working at the Bingley turf research station in Yorkshire. There, he found himself advising several golf courses, notably Southerness in Dumfriesshire. When he subsequently set up his own landscaping business he landed a large contract at Chequers, the Prime Ministerial residence in Buckinghamshire and his reputation as an agronomist grew so quickly that he was asked by the R&A to advise them at all their championship venues from 1972.

Sunningdale Golf Club invited Jim Arthur to pay a visit. In January 1977, a Special General Committee meeting was convened to hear his presentation. Arthur recommended that a policy of more aeration, less watering and less fertilising should be followed. This, he said, was the only way to restore the courses as faster running, with firmer turf and more fescue on the fairways; a course for running golf, rather than target golf.

Jim Arthur. Credit: Fine Golf.

Donald Steel, who was present at the 1977 meeting in his capacity as the Club's consultant course architect, recalls that Jim Arthur's prescriptions were warmly embraced by the Committee. But three and a half years later, in July 1980, a meeting of the General Committee was convened again, "specifically to discuss matters relating to greenkeeping policy in the light of the condition of the course after four years of following the general principles as laid out by our retained adviser J.H. Arthur."

Arthur's methods, which were being faithfully followed by Head Greenkeeper Jack Macmillan and his team, were resulting in the regrowth of bent and fescue grasses on the greens – precisely what they were aiming to achieve. But it was taking time to get rid of all the *poa annua* which did not grow as quickly and did always not reach the cutting height. The result was inconsistent greens, which ran at different speeds in different patches. While the medicine was working, the patient was in a wavering state.

That summer, the Committee acknowledged the annoyance and frustration of "members, committee and staff" at the uneven pace of the greens and conceded defeat in their attempt to restore the greens to 100 per cent bent and fescues. They drew up plans to top dress the greens in the autumn with phosphates, albeit of the organic kind. To promote growth, the greens would be treated with screened sludge and an application of three tons of sulphate of ammonia. However, that autumn, the weather conditions were such that it was considered impractical to top dress the greens.

Despite the Committee's wobble over top dressings, other key aspects of the Jim Arthur prescription – slitting, reducing the application of water and reduced mechanical cultivations – were fully implemented. Jim Arthur, who was doing more at that time than anyone in the country for the development of greenkeeping, was invited back annually to inspect the courses and make recommendations.

He wrote to the Club Secretary Keith Almond in
July 1983:

*First, very many thanks for all your hospitality and
for a very rewarding and interesting day. It is so
pleasant to find everyone on the same wavelength
and none of the clashes of opinion which mar visits
elsewhere! It is no co-incidence that this team-work
has produced lasting first class conditions – it seems
a far cry from the greens which were described in
1976 as "stinking bogs smelling like gas works"!*

*... There are few minor blemishes but Jack knows
exactly what and what to do, but by and large I
thought these greens were as good as or indeed better
than anything I have seen in recent months – a happy
balance between traditional lightening fast heathland
character and the uniformity of colour and texture
which the majority of golfers demand. Despite all the
arguments about true links conditions for the Open
Championships,[41] any Head Greenkeeper must take
into account the fact that the <u>majority</u> of his members
will settle for a happy compromise – but equally if
they want to play full greens 365 days a year, they
must do it the Sunningdale way.*

---

41 The Open was held at Royal Birkdale in 1983.

*The majority of greens are very well aerated, with
good root development and no serious compaction.
Putting surfaces were superbly true and reasonably
fast and very fine textured. Sensible irrigation has
maintained turf density...*

The 1976 drought had led to a new fairway watering system on
both courses being installed in 1978, together with a reservoir
next to the fifteenth fairway on the New Course, installed in
1979. Despite providing seven million gallons of water, Jim
Arthur was concerned in the dry summer of 1983 that supplies
might run out. Another reservoir was built next to the existing
one by the fifteenth hole in 1990 at a cost of £25,000.

Even with this extra capacity, in the hot summer of 1995,
supplies did run out. The Club obtained a licence from the
Environment Agency in October 1997 to sink a borehole on
the Old Course, which allows an additional eleven million
gallons to be drawn.

Jim Arthur's reports did not mince their words. He
was always very supportive of the requests of the Head
Greenkeeper for new equipment and very critical of "such old
fashioned heresies as liming acid fairways – in Heaven's name,
we <u>want</u> them acid, which is what heathland is all about."
He was deeply troubled by seeing over watering and over
fertilising turning too many heathland courses into meadows.

By 1987, in Arthur's opinion, the Green Committee was
making some serious mistakes. For example, in July, they
decided to cut the greens lower, to 1/8 of an inch from 3/16.

The Head Greenkeeper Jack Macmillan advised that this would mean having to use fertiliser, which would in turn encourage meadow grasses; but the Committee wanted the faster greens for July as well as the Autumn Meeting and Founders Foursomes. To Jim Arthur, such a policy represented short term gratification at the expense of long term stewardship.

He visited again that October accompanied by several Committee members. The Green Committee minutes record that "his verbal report had been seriously critical. His written report was awaited. It was discussed whether the Secretary should arrange for a second opinion." When the written report was submitted, the Green Committee, chaired by D.Y. (David) Davies, considered the report "unnecessarily vitriolic, insulting and repetitive" and judged that it had exceeded its brief.

With Jim Arthur's impending retirement[42], the Committee decided that the future of acceptable agronomy lay with Dr Peter Hayes of the STRI, whose report for the Club (written at the same time) reached essentially the same conclusions as Jim Arthur's, only it made its points more politely. The essential Arthur policies remained in place: frequent and thorough aeration, only use organic fertiliser during the growing season, and irrigate when necessary but not to excess.

In the decades since, it has been noted by agronomist reports that swards on the New Course still contain noticeably more *Agrostis*, although *poa annua* is still a

---

42 Jim Arthur retired in 1988 and died on May 14, 2005.

Heathland fire, 2020. Credit: Amphibian and Reptile Conservation (ARC).

significant sward component. Striking a balance between playing on fast greens while not damaging the quality of the sward is the perennial challenge.

Head Greenkeeper Jack Macmillan left the Club in May 1990. Later that summer, a huge heathland fire would sweep across 200 acres of the Club's freehold land. Aside from the "Abysinnia" fire of 1933, fires on Chobham Common were prevalent in the 1950s and 1960s, after which a network of tracks and firebreaks were created. More fires broke out in 2001, 2002, 2010 and most recently in 2020, when a similar wildfire damaged over 100 acres of land adjacent to the course. The fire spread as far as Wentworth causing the abandonment of the final event of the Rose Ladies Series.

CHAPTER 12

Land Lease

In February 1954, the Committee unanimously agreed to
purchase 18 acres of land which had been held on temporary
licence from the Onslow Estate ever since the construction
of the Jubilee in 1934. This land covered the last half of the
majestic sixth hole and the first half of the seventh hole on
the New Course. The price would be £225 plus Solicitors'
and Agents' costs, and a member who wished to remain
unanimous provided £100 towards the purchase price.

Committee member Harry Watney was given
responsibility for overseeing the purchase. In the nick of
time, he realised that the 18 acres that the Club had agreed
to buy did not include all the land covered by the golf course.
A further five acres would be needed. When this oversight
was reported to the Committee in June, the Committee
indicated that they were reluctant to buy any more land if it
could be avoided. A large-scale Ordnance Survey map was
pored over, and it was suggested to Mr Watney that a new
plan be redrawn which still measured 18 acres but which
would now cover the area of the golf holes. Discussions
ensued between the Club's solicitors and the Onslow Estate
Surveyor, but the Committee's attempt to redraw the map did

not work out. In the event, the Club agreed to purchase the full 23 acres.

In December 1966, another land deal was done with the Onslow estate. 193 acres of Chobham Common land beyond the New Course, on which no golf courses sit, were acquired by the Club for £1,000. This land sits to the south east of the course, to the right of the seventh and fifteenth fairways.

A negotiation to consolidate the club's six different leases with St John's College was concluded in 1974 when a sixty year extension was agreed. This was not before the Committee had suggested that the Club should exchange its freehold land of twelve holes of the New Course (the 168 acres of land that the club had purchased in 1922 and 23 acres in 1954 from the Earl of Onslow) in return for a new long lease on favourable terms over the whole property. Over the course of the negotiations with St John's, a subsequent committee rowed back on this proposal and a new deal was reached to consolidate all the St John's leases and extend by sixty years.

With the expiry of the consolidated lease approaching in 2035, preliminary discussions with St John's College began in 2020 over the renewal of the lease. Heads of terms on a new deal, consisting of the exchange of the 12 holes of freehold New Course land owned by the Club in return for a new 125 year lease, were drawn up in early 2022. Opinion amongst Club members towards the deal was divided, so the Committee chose first to make an offer for the freehold title of the land belonging to St John's College; this was rejected by the College which indicated that it wished to remain the long term freeholder.

The Committee then voted (10–5) to recommend the 125 year lease deal to members. A ballot took place and at an EGM on 12 February 2023, the results were announced: 52 per cent of members voted in favour of the deal, 48 per cent against. As the vote required a 75 per cent majority, the deal was not passed. The Club retains its freehold land which includes 12 holes of the New; its lease on six holes of the New Course and all but a small "ransom strip" of the Old is due to expire in 2034.

The Club has investigated many ideas over the past fifty years as to how to make best use of its 193 acres of freehold Chobham Common land which are not currently used for golf. Some members, for example, would love to reopen the abandoned old Colt loop, which would not be too hilly for fitter members and those employing the services of caddies or motorised carts.

In 1973, representatives of the Club met with the Divisional Planning Officer who suggested that an application to use the Chobham Common land for the purpose of golf would be met favourably, but that the construction of a new clubhouse and car park would almost certainly be refused planning consent, as they would intrude upon the landscape. A soil survey was commissioned. This reported that the ground was boggy, which would mean high construction costs.

The Committee investigated building more golf holes again in 1984 and then in 1987, after Surrey County Council's

Planning Committee published a *Review of Golf Facilities* in Surrey which suggested that golf courses were an appropriate use of green belt land. But all of the land at Sunningdale which does not form part of the existing golf courses had been designated as a Site of Special Scientific Interest under the 1949 Countryside Act and 1981 Wildlife Countryside Act, which imposed stringent conditions over what could be done in an area of SSSI. Discussions took place with the Nature Conservancy Council (now Natural England) and despite their sympathetic attitude, they did not believe their statutory duty to protect the SSSI area could be overcome.

Further investigations into building a new golf course on the Chobham Common freehold land were made by the PGA European Tour in 1992, in collaboration with the Club. The idea was to build a championship course on the land which would be a "pay and play" facility open to the public when not being used for professional tournaments. Despite a favourable Environmental Assessment by the Surrey Wildlife Trust, the Conservation Officer of English Nature repeated their view "that the nature conservation case for objecting to the development of a further golf course is very strong." In 1994, the project was shelved.

Sunningdale's golf courses sit on the edge of the Thames Basin Heaths Special Protection Area (SPA). While the woodland is more recent and less established, it is the lowland dry heathland (characterised by ling, bell heather, dwarf gorse and birch), wet valley mires and acid bogland areas which have the highest ecological value. The Arc

(Amphibian and Reptile Conservation) Trust have been
managing the area to the south of the New Course (the
site of the old Colt holes 7, 8 and 9) since 1987. The south
facing aspect of Longdown enables reptile basking, and
all six reptile species native to the UK can be found here.
Adders, grass snakes, common lizards and slow worms are
indigenous populations, while sand lizards were introduced
in 1988 and smooth snakes were reintroduced in 2004. The
area also hosts four significant species of ground nesting
birds – the Dartford Warbler, Nightjar, Stonechat and
Woodlark – all of which are protected by the Wildlife and
Countryside Act 1981.

In England, around one hundred golf courses have all or
part of the course designated as SSSI, and in Scotland around
thirty courses have the same designation. Almost all received
their SSSI designations while they were in use as golf courses.
Machrihanish Dunes, a David Maclay Kidd design which
opened in 2009 and has been hailed for its "outstanding
commitment to sustainable golf"[43] is the only course ever to
be constructed on an existing SSSI. For the old Colt holes to
be reopened or new ones put in place on the Sunningdale's
SSSI land, the Club would have to obtain the consent of
Natural England by demonstrating how the changes could
support and improve the habitats of the unique species
currently living in the protected areas.

---

43 By the Association of Golf Tour Operators.

CHAPTER 13

Heathland Revival

After the proliferation of trees across the course in the 1950s and 1960s had taken hold, removing and trimming trees became a standard feature of winter course maintenance work. This work was aimed primarily at preserving tree health and preventing trees from interfering too much with play.

In both 1979 and 1980, for example, trees on the left and right of the 16th fairway were removed, and the Green Committee authorised the removal of trees from the copse beyond the pond and on the right of the 15th to create a clear view to the reservoir. The edge of the woods on the 8th and 9th fairways was also tidied that year. The winter of 1981 saw the thinning of the woods by the 15th fairway, the cutting back of trees to the left of 18th for 100 yards from the tee and the removal of the bottom branches from the pine trees on the left of that fairway.

Each year the trimming and thinning continued until, in 1992, the first extensive programme of tree clearance for over fifty years began on the New Course. The point of taking out trees was to let in light and air, so that large tracts of heather could be regenerated. In turn this would make significant improvements to the drainage of the course.

A team of arborists, Woodcare, explained in their report that heather could be best maintained by mowing, strimming and spraying the grass around it before the grass came into seed, as well as by taking out the birch, oak and pine saplings and spraying their stumps. Maintaining good growing conditions for the grass areas meant keeping the right balance of tree species. Their recommendation was: 80 per cent Scot's pine, 15 per cent birch and oak and 5 per cent others (Rowan tree, Sweet chestnut and shrubs like holly, yew, gorse and broom).

Much of the tree work was carried out by the Club's own staff. That winter, significant forestry clearance took place on the ninth, tenth and 13th of the New and was followed up with a series of trial beds for the restoration of heather. The plan thereafter was to take out a small number of trees once a year rather than a larger number every four or five years.

In spite of this, in the years that followed, trees continued to encroach upon the course. It was widely acknowledged at that time that the New Course was kept in a slightly shabbier condition than the Old, with saplings and large patches of grass regularly appearing in the heather. The general view amongst the membership was that the course was simply not the match of the Old: 65 per cent of all games of golf at the Club were played on the Old. With the Old hosting all the big tournaments at Sunningdale, there was a sense in which the New was still playing second fiddle to its older brother.

As Chairman of the Green Committee in 1999, G.O. (Geoffrey) Vero proposed that a photographic record be set up for each hole from fixed points and at the same time each year. He stressed the strategic threat of the encroachment of trees and the invasion of self-seeding scrub. This, he declared, had to be addressed now and dramatically. Four categories of clearance were identified: routine annual shrub and scrub clearance; thinning of trees for more light and air; lopping or removal of specific trees encroaching onto the line of shot or otherwise adversely affecting playing areas; and felling of trees to encourage heather regeneration and to restore vistas that have been lost. The Committee agreed to embark upon a ten year tree clearance programme.

Course Manager Brian Turner reported in April 2001 that "the heather regeneration work, and tree and scrub clearance has been a success." Further clearance within the wood between holes six, seven and eight would take place the following winter.

In 1999, the oak tree at the 18th green of the New was struck by lightning. Bob Taylor of STRI recommended that a tree bolt be installed to prevent the branch from splitting away from the trunk. But the fix was only temporary. In February 2002, the Sunningdale Secretary Stewart Zuill reported to the Green Committee that the tree had deteriorated and that there was a danger of its limbs falling off. For two long years, members of the Committee agonised over what to do. When Stephen Toon took over as Secretary in 2004, the tree was miraculously still standing, and a tree specialist was called in to provide further diagnosis. The answer that came back was that the tree's health was so precarious that at any moment the tree might not only fall over but shatter into many pieces, giving anyone standing underneath it no time at all to escape. The immediate decision was taken to remove it.

In 2006, two key appointments were made by the Green Committee to continue the effort to improve the quality of the New Course. The first was that of Murray Long as Course Manager. He was given a clear brief to make sure that the greens on <u>both</u> courses were similar to the practice putting green (which is used by players before teeing off on either course) but also to recapture the open heathland character of the New Course. His team took out numerous trees, notably on the short fifth and tenth holes, allowing in more sunlight and airflow to assist the regrowth of heather and finer grasses and enabling the golfer to glimpse attractive views towards other fairways through the trees.

The tree clearances also included the removal of many of the birches and pines that sat along the inside of the dogleg of the sixth hole, which served no purpose other than to undermine the tremendous scale and vista of the hole from the tee. In the years since those tree clearances, the heather has returned in force.

The second appointment was a new consultant architect, in the form of Martin Hawtree, an acknowledged expert on the work of Colt, and whose father and grandfather were course designers. In addition to overseeing the tree clearance work, Hawtree initiated a bunker renewal programme and reshaped the approaches to the New Course's seventeenth and eighteenth holes.

The approach to the seventeenth green was made more rugged, heather was reintroduced, and a higher green constructed, protected by deeper pot bunkers to the right and a steeper bank to the left, with a small 'bail out' zone short of the green. By common consent, caddies now see more missed putts on the subtle slopes of the newly constructed green.

The changes to the eighteenth were more radical still. The path from the first green to the second tee was rerouted to enable the eighteenth tee to be moved backwards onto a higher platform. This made for a more attractive downhill tee shot involving a risk/ reward feature whereby the closer to the right hand trees the ball is hit, the greater the chance of the ball landing on a part of the fairway from where it will shoot forward another twenty yards or so. The approach to the green was dug up, with new deeper bunkers protecting access to the green, which was again reconstructed on higher ground at such a step angle that some members now feel it is too steep, given the high speeds on the stimp-meter which can be achieved today.

A larger, wider first tee was created, so that the first fairway of the New could serve as a practice ground for future professional events, such as the 2008 Women's British Open and the 2009 Senior Open, when the club's own practice ground was being used as a temporary car park.

A project which began in 1990 to restore bunkers on the New Course to their original shape and size has proved not to be as easy as imagined. Photos of original Colt bunkers indicate how much more natural they were compared to the sharp lines favoured by many modern greenkeepers. Just two years after the then Course Manager was given permission by the Green Committee to use his discretion to put back the bunkers to their original condition, the same Course Manager reported that he was revetting some bunkers on the New. Yet revetting is not a practice associated with Colt bunkers. Colt's 1923 bunkers (constructed using horses by Claude Harris) looked more natural and were mostly built into existing hillocks, with sand merging with rough grass and heather at the edges. It is notable that none were rivetted nor held in place by railway sleepers, as they were not designed to be too steep faced.

In recent years, each winter has seen more bunker renewal work on the course. This has often involving more digging

The shape of the original Colt bunker on the left of the fourth green, 1923.

and more bank-building, to create more of a test in the era of the 60 degree wedge. The result is that the bunkering style is not consistent throughout the course. It remained a subject of active debate in recent decades as to whether it is desirable that they should be similar, and in which style they should be maintained.

It is tempting for the modern greenkeeper to produce a perfectly manicured, green, tree-lined course that is pristine in every respect. On some 'made for TV' courses, they even use chlorine to bleach the bunkers. The New Course was not designed to be like this. Over the century of its existence, its founding features have been diluted, but the aim of most Green Committees at Sunningdale has been to keep the course true to its origins: open, rugged and heathery, with wide and angled fairways leading to relatively small greens.

An example of this in practice is the tree removal work that took place on the fourth hole in the winter of 2022. To preserve the course's openness, several trees were removed from the right hand side. Before they were removed, strategic options from the tee had become so restricted that that even the shorter hitter had to shape the ball from left to right just to keep their drive on the fairway. The tee shot is today played to the angled fairway which Colt laid out, but without the deep bunker to the centre-right of the fairway which caught the scratch player's off-line shot in Colt's time. The prevailing wind, thick heather on either side of the fairway, a ditch on the right, and a high green remain part of the hole's defensive armoury.

The distance that the modern golf ball travels provides the same headache for the golfing authorities of today as it did at the end of the 1920s when John Low was campaigning in vain for the distance of the ball to be limited and when Tom Simpson was being asked to redesign courses to make them more mentally challenging. The New Course has always been a real test for the amateur handicap player but the improvements to golf club and ball technology that have taken place in recent decades have made it somewhat easier.

Green committees have responded to this by making use of the vast tract of land on which the New is situated by lengthening holes. More teeing grounds are a development which Colt might have welcomed. "On any course it will be a vital necessity to have a considerable range of teeing-grounds," wrote Colt "so that each hole can be readily lengthened or shortened according to the state of ground, and the strength and direction of the wind. This is a simple precaution which is often disregarded, and even at clubs where ample teeing-grounds exist, it is quite common to find that no intelligent use is made of them."

In a *Memories of Sunningdale*[44] interview with Bruce Critchley in 2023, Gary Player indicated that he favoured committees putting in more forwards and backwards tees – to cater for all types of player. At Sunningdale, new forward tees were built on the Old Course in 2022. They have not yet

---

44 https://www.youtube.com/watch?v=gDABHPoT1s4. 9m30s.

appeared on the New. Harry Colt saw no point in making weaker players make compulsory carries from the tee, not least to save beginners "a great many niblick shots" and so they could keep up with play:

> *"From the ordinary tees, however, it will be found inadvisable to arrange many compulsory carries which greatly exceed 110 yards… A few good players may hold that this is a piece of special pleading on behalf of the duffer, but the majority even of those would probably agree that they do not enjoy additional pleasure on courses where long compulsory carries are the rule rather than the exception."*

Tom Simpson's response to the length that the ball was travelling was to adopt every means within the architect's power "to twist the Tiger's tail" by increasing the "intricacies that already exist". The intricacies favoured by Simpson take the form of dead ground, camouflage, the removal of marks at which the good player can aim, to keep the surface "keen and slippery", and to allow there to be no absolute way to open the hole, so that the choice of what line to play is always a choice of evils.

"To manoeuvre him into two minds is analogous to the bowler's wish to beat the batsman by keeping him guessing, since any state of indecision is likely to prove fatal," wrote

Simpson. He would not have approved of today's rangefinder, GPS and laser distance-measuring technology.

The debates over to how best to adapt courses, at a time when technology is making the game easier for all standards of player, have been forever with us. It has been possible to adapt the courses because of the improvements in technology and numbers of green staff that have been made available to successive Course Managers. Lawson Bingham had 16 staff covering both courses in 1992. Brian Turner had 22 green staff in 2000.

Climate change has made its impact on the courses. To create closely mown, fast greens at a time when the summers are getting warmer, in recent years the greens have been regularly overseeded with new varieties of grasses to ensure they are resistant to drought conditions. But still the fundamental Jim Arthur principles – of aeration, using only organic fertilisers and watering only sparingly – are followed; and they have proved to be as environmentally responsible as he always claimed they were.

While the New Course is presented in good condition on almost every day of the year, Sunningdale members still aspire to ever higher standards of maintenance. Philip Carr, a retired schoolmaster and multiple Club Gold Medal winner, who retired as Chair of the Green Committee in 2023, observed that, in his four years in the role, he received more letters from Club members about their golf courses than he ever received in his entire career from parents about their children. Such is the affection in which Sunningdale is held!

CHAPTER 14

Golf on the New

"I can't think of a place in the world that would be nicer to be, and more pleasant to be, a member than this course. If you are an elderly member, you have got the Old Course. If you are a young man, you have got the New Course. The New course, in my opinion, is one of the twenty best in the world... when the heather is in bloom there is nothing to beat the New Course."

Gary Player, in conversation with Bruce Critchley, 2023.

Sunningdale's most famous visitor from America in its early years came from Brookline, Massachusetts. Francis Ouimet won the US Open Champion as an amateur in 1913 and was the first non-Briton to become Captain of the R&A in 1951. He is credited with bringing golf into the American sporting mainstream long before the rise of legends such as Bobby Jones, Arnold Palmer, Jack Nicklaus and Tiger Woods.

Forty years later, Sunningdale welcomed an exchange student Zarka Smith, also from Brookline, Massachusetts, onto the green staff to study turf research. She had been in the country for three months and had just two weeks to go before she returned to her parents' home in the USA,

US Open champion Francis Ouimet playing the Old at Sunningdale, 1914.

before she tragically died in a motorcycle road accident
on 17 September, 1992. A member of staff at the golf club
identified the body. A maple tree, which sits between the
third and fifteenth fairways, was planted in her memory.
Of all the trees on the New Course at Sunningdale, this
shines the brightest through the seasons.

In 1923, the Sunningdale member would either arrive at
the village railway station or by car. His chauffeur could go
and play the Nine Hole on Titlarks Hill and be back in time
to drive him home. Caddiemaster Jimmy Sheridan would
be on hand to allocate a caddie to carry the bag. During the
Great War, most caddies were girls but by 1923, boys and
men were again filling the ranks.

Starting players from the first tee at the weekend would
be Jimmie Davidson. The nephew of a local builder who had
served an apprenticeship in the family firm as a carpenter, he
was known for his impeccable honesty, refusing any attempts
by members to buy times from him, while constantly

inventing new ways to regulate the flow of golfers and caddies. One way to obtain a time was for golfers to place their ball "into the slot", the Club Committee reiterating in 1930 that the ball must be put down only by the player and not by a Caddie or a friend.

HRH the Prince of Wales, who became King Edward VIII in 1936, was Captain in 1930.

After retiring as starter, Jimmie Davidson continued to caddy and to apply his carpentry skills to the manufacture of shoe racks, lockers, tables and benches for the course. He is said to have inherited a good legacy from a wealthy relative, but Caddiemaster Jimmy Sheridan felt this proved his undoing, encouraging a penchant for ale and horses which outlasted his available cash.

Also fond of a beverage[45] was Mr Jack White, resident professional and winner of the Open Championship at Sandwich in 1904. He or one of his half dozen club-making staff would be on hand to regrip a club or fix any broken hickory shafts or loose clubheads.

---

45 Jack White regrettably lost his job as Sunningdale's Professional in 1926 after a drunken incident.

Occasionally, a golfer might catch a glimpse of royalty across the open fairways. David, the Prince of Wales (who was later to become Edward VIII) joined the club in 1924 and became Captain in 1930.

His younger brother Bertie, Duke of York (who was later to become George VI) became Captain of the club in 1932. Each royal brother managed to get their handicap down into single figures; the Prince of Wales played off 6. Jimmy Sheridan became firm friends with both future kings, who would maintain a measure of royal distance from members by changing their shoes in his office.

> "Which course am I using today?" the Prince of Wales asked Sheridan early in his golfing career.
>
> "The New Course, Sir."
>
> "But, dammit, Sheridan, you know I prefer the Old Course."
>
> "Ay, Sir, but the New Course is wider," came the response from Sheridan.

For many years, the Club's President was HRH Prince Arthur, Duke of Connaught and Strathearn. The seventh child and third son of Queen Victoria, he died aged 91 in 1942. He was succeeded by the 17th Earl of Derby, after whose death in 1948 the position was abolished.

The first recorded hole in one on the New Course was by the Club's Founder T.A. (Tom) Roberts. Playing with

HRH the Duke and Duchess of York were Captains of Sunningdale and Sunningdale Ladies' Clubs respectively in 1932.

E.B. Road and C.F. Yeomans on Saturday 8 August 1925, he holed his tee shot at the 186 yard 17th hole.

In 1930, dogs were permitted to accompany their owners on the golf course for the first time, but only on weekdays. They were strictly forbidden from the clubhouse. This was the year that Cadets between the ages of 14 and 20 were allowed to play on payment of an annual subscription (of one guinea). They were allowed in the clubhouse, on weekdays.

The New was used for occasional matches and tournaments, often in conjunction with the Old. Shortly before the Simpson redesign, on 24 April 1934, the Guildford alliance championship final was played on both the Old and the New. H.B. Rhodes of Wentworth beat A.E. Matthews of the Berkshire, with scores of 74 and 76 over the Old and New courses respectively.

After the war, the club was in financial difficulties, and it is said that Gerald Micklem, along with A.C. Critchley and Norman Hamilton Smith,[46] spent some of his personal fortune propping it up. Gerald Micklem worked hard to recruit some of the best amateur players in southern England to join the Club in the post-war years. While Sunningdale was already the home of Philp Scrutton and Bruce Critchley, Walker Cup players such as Laddie Lucas, Max McCready, John Langley, Ian Caldwell, Guy Wolstenhome, David Frame, Roddy Carr, John Davies and Michael King all joined Sunningdale – like Micklem, having learned the game at other clubs. Sunningdale became a club where high quality golf was played, and often for high stakes.

Shortly after the reopening of the New in 1950, it was decided that the Club would host the £2000 Daks Professional Tournament on both the Old and the New courses the following year. It was won by the Scottish professional golf champion John Panton, of Glenbervie, who had recently returned from a tour of South Africa. He won first prize of £400 after carding a 72 hole total of 282, three strokes ahead of Bobby Locke and five strokes ahead of Sunningdale's own professional Arthur Lees. The victory

---

46 An interest free loan of £500 from Norman Hamilton Smith was recorded in the Committee minutes of 13 May 1950. He became a Trustee of the Club.

secured Panton a place in the Great Britain and Ireland team in the Ryder Cup played at Pinehurst No 2 the following year. Later in life, John Panton became the R&A's professional. He is the only golfer other than Arnold Palmer to have a drink[47] named after him.

Sunningdale's Old Course hosted the Golf Illustrated Gold Vase five times between 1910 and 1948 but in 1952[48] this famous amateur tournament was played for the first time on the New. British Walker Cup player John Langley beat his nearest rival, the American amateur Dick Chapman (who had won at Sunningdale in 1948), with a morning 72 and an afternoon 68 – a new, New Course record. Langley went on to win the Gold Vase again in 1953, played again over the New Course. Although he played out of Stoke Poges, John Langley was also a Sunningdale member who chaired the Sunningdale Green Committee in the 1950s.

Ever since the Haskell ball saw the creation of golf balls with a rubber core, the Dunlop Tyre company had been involved in the manufacture of golf balls. After the war they sponsored the Dunlop 2000 Guineas Tournament, a five round stroke play event played over both Sunningdale courses open to professionals. In 1952 the first prize was £350, won by Max Faulkner (Hindhead) with a combined

---

47 A John Panton is made with bitters, lime and ginger beer, while an Arnold Palmer is made with iced tea and lemonade.

48 The Golf Illustrated Gold Vase would be hosted by Sunningdale for each of the next 21 years after 1952.

score of 345 (68,73, 67,65, 72), the lowest total since the tournament started.

In the final round on the New Course, Faulkner was out in 41 strokes. On the tenth tee, he needed to be back in 38 strokes to beat TB Haliburton who had finished with 352. He came back in 31 strokes including six birdies. His figures on the back nine were: 3 4 4 4 2 4 4 2 4. Faulkner's win at Sunningdale completed what the newspapers called the 'treble'; the previous year, Faulkner had won the Open Championship at Royal Portrush and the Dunlop Masters tournament at Wentworth.

Open Champion Max Faulkner won 2000 Guineas Tournament at Sunningdale in 1952.

In 1956 the Dunlop Tournament returned to Sunningdale and was also played over both courses. Sunningdale's Professional Arthur Lees and Gary Player, playing together in the fourth round, each scored birdie threes at the difficult ninth hole on the New. The 20 year old South African set the professional course record with a 64 and went on to win the tournament, with a total of 338, two strokes ahead of Lees, and won £500.

The amateur course record for the New was next broken in the Gold Vase in 1958, when Michael Lunt returned a 65. It remained in place for 35 years until 1993, when it was

Clive Clark won the Gold Vase as an amateur in 1965. A year later,
he became Sunningdale's touring professional.

broken three times in one day, again in the Gold Vase: first,
by J Lomas of Woodcote Park with a 64, then by Van Phillips
of Stoke Poges with a 63, and finally by Charles Challen, also
of Stoke Poges, with a 62.

Nineteen year old Clive Clark of Ganton won the 1965
Gold Vase with a brilliant 36 hole total of 139 strokes.
His first round on the New Course included a 6 and a 7
but he still managed to take only 70 strokes. John Tullis
and Bruce Critchley of Sunningdale both finished in the
top ten, six strokes behind Clark. The victory secured
Clark his place in the Walker Cup team in Baltimore later
that year, after which he turned professional, playing out
of Sunningdale from 1966 onwards. In 1975, he became
the Sunningdale Club Professional.

The fantastic tales that have been told at Sunningdale of rounds played over the New Course over the past century are legion. One that does not purport to be true was the round played by James Bond in the opening chapter of the James Bond continuation novel Colonel Sun, written by Kingsley Amis under the pseudonym Robert Markham and published by Jonathan Cape in 1968.

In 2000, the centenary year of the formation of the club, Shell's Wonderful World of Golf came to Sunningdale to film a match over the New Course between Gary Player and Jack Nicklaus. Challenge matches between two professional golfers, attended by a small gallery of interested spectators, with a purse put up by a wealthy benefactor or company sponsor, have their roots at the beginnings of the professional game. The Shell sponsorship enabled a television audience to watch as if they themselves were out on the course, with conversations taking place between the players in between shots. On this occasion, the purse was $150,000, the match was 18 holes of strokeplay and Peter Alliss provided the interviews and commentary. Nicklaus won with a four under par 67 to Player's even par 71.

On 9 July 2023, in the centenary year of the New Course, another match between leading professionals of the day was played between Tommy Fleetwood and Justin Rose, one of the club first professional members. The match was played in a stroke play format over 18 holes on the New in front of a crowd of members and their guests as well as the assembled media. Rose carded a very solid 65 but was beaten in the end by Fleetwood's 63, just one shot shy of Graeme Storm's course record. The match was captured by the cameras of Sky Sports and compered by former Ryder Cup Captain and Sunningdale member Paul McGinley. The highlights of the match were broadcast on 26 July 2023 and in subsequent weeks.

Played over both courses at Sunningdale every year is the Critchley Salver, a 36 hole scratch Women's Open, which was inaugurated in 1982 to recognise the legacy of Diana Critchley at Sunningdale Golf Club. Before she married Brigadier Critchley in 1938, Diana Fishwick won the British Ladies Amateur Championship in 1930 at Formby at the age of 19 and represented Great Britain and Ireland in the Curtis Cup in 1932 at Wentworth and in 1934 at Chevy Chase, Maryland. In 1950, she captained the Curtis Cup team against the US in Buffalo New York. Along with Joan Cooper and Hersey Langley, she established the Ladies Section of Sunningdale Golf Club in the same year and, for many years afterwards, Diana Critchley served as Hon Secretary of the Ladies Section.

Since 2018 the Critchley Salver at Sunningdale has been combined with the Astor Salver at The Berkshire to create the Critchley Astor Salver. Both events are run separately with their own prizes, but the combined totals over 72 holes enable players to earn world ranking points. The 2015 edition resulted in victory for 17 year old Lizzie Prior who won by two shots after shooting a course record of eight under par 67 on the New Course.

In the men's amateur game, world ranking points can be earned by entering the Gerald Micklem Cup. Inaugurated in 1998 in memory of Sunningdale's greatest golfing ambassador of the second half of the twentieth century, it is open to men over the age of 35 and played as a scratch medal over 54 holes on the New Course. After 36 holes, the top 20 and ties make the cut to the final 18 holes.

Each year, the Sunningdale Foursomes receives entries from

Lizzie Prior receives the Critchley Salver from Bruce Critchley, 2015. The Salver is named after his mother Diana, who was British champion, Curtis Cup player and Sunningdale member.

leading golfers, amateur and professional, all of whom have impressive golfing CVs and some of whom have played on the PGA & European Tours, in the Ryder or Walker Cup or have won Major Championships.

The Foursomes was first played in 1934 and is today played by 128 pairs over both the Old and New Courses in the first or second week of March. On the six occasions that it was played before World War Two, it was one four times by a mixed partnership. Diana Fishwick (later Critchley) and Noel Layton won the first ever trophy, followed by New Course designer

John Morrison and Joyce
Wethered (Lady Amory) who
won in the next two years. In
1938, Alf Padgham won with
Pam Barton, the Curtis Cup
player who lost her life aged
26 while serving as an RAF
Auxiliary in 1943.

Diana Fishwick with Grand Slam winner
Bobby Jones in 1930. She won the British
Ladies Amateur Golf Championship in
the same year.

In 1955, the year she
won the Girls Amateur
Championship, 17 year
old Angela Ward (later
Bonallack) and Cambridge
University's Robin O'Brien
were the youngest couple
to play in the event. A triple
blue in hockey, cricket and
golf, O'Brien was a first class Irish cricketer who tragically died
of leukemia in 1959. The film actor and Sunningdale member
Michael Medwin, who died in 2020 aged 96 also played in the
event that year. He later claimed that he had given his name
to the grass hollow to the immediate left of the second green
on the New Course behind the hillock. "We call it Medwin's
Mellow," he said, "because I always end up there."

In 1958, the tournament began with a record entry of
132 pairs, with both the Old and the New Course being used
on the first two days. The famous names on the champions
board of post-war winners suggests that the event is worthy

of a book of its own. Max Faulkner, Peter Alliss, Michael Bonallack, Bruce Critchley, Neil Coles, Peter Benka, Peter Oosterhuis, John Davies, Michael King, John Putt, Clive Clark, Michael Hughesdon, Maureen Madill, Sam Torrance, Ronan Rafferty, Roger Chapman, Anthony Wall, Luke Donald and Julie Hall are all notable twentieth century winners, while mother and son combination Carol and Richard Caldwell were the first twentieth century champions.

In its centenary year, 2023 saw the opening round of the Sunningdale Foursomes played on the New Course. Regrettably, the competition was abandoned after round one on account of heavy snowfall. It was abandoned for the same reason in 2018 and because of the Covid-19 pandemic in 2020.

From 2004 to 2013, Europe's International Final Qualifying tournament for the Open Championship was held over both the Old and New Courses at Sunningdale. Would-be qualifiers for the Open were required to play 36 holes in a day, a format very familiar to professionals of yesteryear but rare in the modern professional game. In the first event, held in 2004, to keep the field moving, the competitors went out in two balls, with the fastest players sent out early to set the pace. Colin Montgomerie and Gordon Brand Jr were thrilled to be given early start times and to be able play quickly. The event always produced an exciting climax as dusk fell, with competitors tied for the last remaining places playing off over extra holes on the New for a coveted place in the Open.

Englishman Graeme Storm holds the professional course record on the New Course, a morning 62 recorded during the Open Championship International Final Qualifying in 2009. Combined with an excellent afternoon round of 68 on Sunningdale's Old Course, he comfortably qualified to play in the Open, which was the last time the Championship was played at Turnberry.

Three years later, in 2012, the New Course record was matched by Welshman Jamie Donaldson in the same event. He qualified for the Open in third place behind James Morrison, a 26 year old English amateur from nearby Chertsey, who carded a six under par 63 on the New. That year was the last time the Open was played at Royal Lytham & St Annes.

Brooks Koepka, who has gone on to win five majors and become world number one, won the event in 2013. He attributed his 65 and 68 to the quality of his putting, having felt like he was in the heather all day. That year was the 16th and most recent time that the Open Championship was played at Muirfield, a course described by Paul McGinley that day as "the strongest of the all the Open venues"[49].

Many club competitions are played each year by the Sunningdale membership on the New Course. The Arthur Lees Masters Salver (fourball better ball), Arthur Lees Irish Medal (three ball better ball) and the Family Trophy (foursomes) are open to all genders; the Men's and Women's Member Guest Days (fourball and foursomes); the Dunedin Cup (individual men's handicap medal) and Robert Sweeney

---

49 https://www.youtube.com/watch?v=1Nrsuq2_pzY&t=51s.

Challenge Trophies (individual men's scratch and handicap medal) are played over 18 holes of the New; while the John Langley is played over 18 holes of the New and 18 holes of the Old in a single day. The names of some of the past winners of these events read like a roll call of some of England's finest amateurs of their day.

The New's centenary was marked by the hosting of the leading amateur event, the Brabazon Trophy, on the course in May 2023. It was won by Liam Nolan of Ireland with a final round 68 after previous rounds of 72, 70 and 67, to finish at three under par. "The name and history of Sunningdale Golf Club makes it one of the coolest places to win a tournament," he remarked afterwards.

A sketch of H.S. Colt by Charles Ambrose.

"The real test of a course," wrote Colt, "is not 'Does it provide a test for the game?' but 'Will it live?'" Colt's New Course at Sunningdale underwent some significant surgery in its younger years but, a hundred years on, this creation of nature is very much alive. From the Golden Age to the present day, it has stood the test of time.

Bibliography and online sources

Course-Constructor Colt and His Masterpiece, Charles Ambrose, The Motor Owner, 1922

Creating Classics, The Golf Courses of Harry Colt, Peter Pugh and Harry Lord, Icon Books, 2005

Critch! The Memoirs of Brigadier-General AC Critchley CMG, CBE, DSO, Hutchinson, 1961

finegolf.co.uk

Gerald Micklem, A Life in Golf, John Littlewood, Grant Books, Worcestershire, 2014

Golf Courses as Designed Landscapes of Historic Interest, EIGCA Report 42, Historic England, 2017

golfclubatlas.com

golfchronicle.wordpress.com

Masters of Design, Henry Lord and Peter Pugh, Icon Books, 2009

My Life and Soft Times, Henry Longhurst, Cassell, London 1971

Sheridan of Sunningdale, by Jimmy Sheridan, Country Life Ltd, London 1967

Simpson & Co. Golf Architects, by Fred Hawtree, Rhod McEwan, 2016

Some Essays on Golf Architecture, by HS Colt and CH Alison, Grant Books, Worcestershire, 1993

Sunningdale Golf Club Archive:
Committee Minutes 1900–1953
Suggestions Book 1900–2000
Green Committee Minutes 1953–2000

Sunningdale Golf Club, Official Handbook, by Robert Browning, Golf Clubs Association, 1950

The Architectural Side of Golf, by HN Wethered and T Simpson, Grant Books, Worcestershire, 1995

The Game of Golf, Horace Hutchison and Tom Simpson, Joyce and Roger Wethered, Bernard Darwin, Seeley Service and Co., London, 1931.

The History of Sunningdale Golf Club 1900–2000, by John Whitfield, Sunningdale Golf Club, 2000

The Sunningdale Golf Club, by Bernard Darwin, Golf Clubs Association, London 1924

The Sunningdale Story, by Guy Bennett 1962, Ed. John Churchill, 2012

The Rolex World's Top 1000 Golf Courses, by D'Algue Selection, Gaëtan Mourgue d'Algue, et al, 2012

thefriedegg.com